History of the Township of
Mount Pleasant
Wayne County
Pennsylvania

A
Discourse
Delivered on
Thanksgiving Day
November 22, 1855

Rev. Samuel Whaley

HERITAGE BOOKS
2010

HERITAGE BOOKS
AN IMPRINT OF HERITAGE BOOKS, INC.

Books, CDs, and more—Worldwide

For our listing of thousands of titles see our website
at
www.HeritageBooks.com

A Facsimile Reprint
Published 2010 by
HERITAGE BOOKS, INC.
Publishing Division
100 Railroad Ave. #104
Westminster, Maryland 21157

Copyright © 2003 Heritage Books, Inc.

Originally Published by M. W. Dodd
No. 59 Chambers Street
New York
1856

— Publisher's Notice —
In reprints such as this, it is often not possible to remove blemishes from the original. We feel the contents of this book warrant its reissue despite these blemishes and hope you will agree and read it with pleasure.

International Standard Book Numbers
Paperbound: 978-0-7884-2315-4
Clothbound: 978-0-7884-8461-2

CORRESPONDENCE.

MOUNT PLEASANT, Nov. 26, 1855.

TO THE REV. SAMUEL WHALEY :

Dear Sir :—We had the pleasure, in common with your other hearers, in listening to the Historical Discourse delivered by you on last Thanksgiving Day. We feel that the facts therein embodied must have cost much patient labor and research, and are of interest to us, and well worthy to be transmitted to future generations. We therefore request that you would furnish a copy of it for publication.   Yours very truly,   WILLIAM R. STONE,
URIEL WRIGHT,
HENRY W. BROWN,
JOHN F. SHERWOOD,
WILLIAM WRIGHT,
ELDAD ATWATER,
EDWARD M. ATWATER.

MOUNT PLEASANT, July, 1856.

Gentlemen :—In furnishing a copy of my "Historical Discourse" for publication, it is due to state that the collection of these facts was made with no other intention than the gratification of a love of such incidents. These facts accumulated in a few years to such a number, and possessed such a degree of interest, that the thought of a historical discourse was suggested. From that time my object has been to form an accurate narrative of events in the order of time in which they occurred. This was found to be a work of much more labor than that of collecting isolated facts. The principal difficulties have arisen, (1) from a want of suitable records. A few of the first settlers were in the habit of making brief notes of events, which have been of great service. Many of the facts, however, are from eye-witnesses. Difficulties have also (2) arisen from indistinct memory—(3) conflicting accounts—and (4) from the death of some who were familiar with the early history of the settlement.

Since receiving your note requesting its publication, much additional matter has been added to it, and some corrections made which have been kindly suggested by those who heard it. In its present form it is much enlarged, and will be of much more value as a book of historical reference. It has been my great object to give a lucid, correct, and impartial narrative. That inaccuracies have crept into it, would be folly to deny. If the long delay in furnishing the manuscript needs further apology, it will be sufficient to say, that the author has ever regarded its preparation as secondary to his professional duties. Having charge of a large parish, little time could be devoted to this work. He has also had an unusual demand upon his time and efforts since its delivery.

It has been said by a distinguished historian of this State, that "concerning the early settlement of this county, little has been preserved." Hoping that this discourse may furnish some materials for a future history of this county, encourage similar efforts in other localities, and promote the interests of intelligence and truth—I herewith furnish you the manuscript.

    Very truly
     Your friend and fellow-citizen,
          SAMUEL WHALEY.

WILLIAM R. STONE, and others.

DISCOURSE.

"HEAR this, ye old men, and give ear all ye inhabitants of the land. Hath this been in your days, or even in the days of your fathers? Tell ye your children of it, and let your children tell their children, and their children another generation."
—Joel i. 2, 3.

WITH these words the prophet Joel opens the narrative of events contained in his prophecy. These events were even then transpiring, or about to transpire. They were matters of great interest and importance to all the people. He appeals to the old men whether such events as were about to take place ever occurred in their days, or in the days of their fathers. They are such as should and would be remembered. They affected the whole land, and were of interest to all the people. The prophet, therefore, requires that they should be related repeatedly, and handed down from one generation to another.

The importance of historical narratives was understood at a very early day. Events of a public and important nature, were in various ways carefully preserved: these formed a ground of admonition and instruction. It is, therefore, a duty incumbent upon us, who have so much greater facilities to record the events of the past, for the benefit of those yet to come upon the stage of action. Let me then invite your attention to the history of this *Township*, which is the object of this discourse. I shall introduce it by directing your attention to its

I. NATURAL FEATURES.

The township of Mount Pleasant lies in a territory broken into hills and valleys, by the extreme northern branches of the Alleghany range of mountains. This range is here lost in the irregularities of the surface. The only mountain in this town worthy a name, is the Moosic range, which here runs North and South, and receives upon its summit our Western boundary. In its natural state it is covered with a heavy growth of beech, maple, and hemlock, with a limited quantity of ash and elm interspersed. The soil is chiefly a sandy loam, and rests on a strata of sand rock, called "Millstone Grit." At various places the old red sandstone appears, giving character to the soil.* The most prominent streams of this town are the Dyberry † and the Lackawaxen. The former runs through the Eastern, and the latter through the Western part of the town, furnishing upon their banks many valuable mill-seats.

There are in this town four of those beautiful lakes so often found in this part of the State. They are formed by springs, and are clear as crystal. They usually constitute the head of some stream. The names of these lakes are as follows: Duck Lake, Rock Lake, Howe's Pond, and Bigelow Lake. The first two mentioned are in the northeast part of

* See Appendix, No. 4. † See Appendix, No. 5.

the town, and divided by the town line. Howe's Pond has two outlets. One is at the Eastern extremity, and empties into the Dyberry. The other is at the Western extremity, and empties into the Lackawaxen. Bigelow Lake forms the head of Thompson's Creek, which also flows into the Lackawaxen. This stream, a few rods below the lake, plunges over a fall of about one hundred feet, in two perpendicular cataracts, which are but a few feet apart. We know of no waterfall in this region equal to it in beauty. The view from below is enchanting. The shrubbery and trees which overhang the crystal water as it dashes over the rocks, greatly add to its effect. We hope the enterprising individual who has erected his mills by the side of this waterfall, will suffer them long to remain.

II. ABORIGINES.

There are no evidences within the limits of this town of any Indian battle-ground, or any important event connected with their history. Still there are abundant indications that it was once occupied by them as a hunting-ground.

The large number of Indian arrow-heads found here, leaves no room to doubt it.* These arrow-heads are invariably made of flint. This region afforded for them a rich field. On the head waters of the Dy-

---

* There have also been found in this vicinity, pieces of ancient English coin. One now in possession of the writer bears date 1757, coined under George II., King of Great Britain.

berry there was undoubtedly an Indian encampment. There are still to be seen scars on the sugar-maple there, which, at the time the first settlers came, indicated great age. These, from their appearance, are supposed to have been made by the aborigines, for the sap. There is also in the same vicinity, a natural opening on the rich alluvial soil of this stream, where it is supposed they cultivated a little Indian corn.

There were also a large quantity of Beaver, as well as other kinds of deer, which furnished an extensive field for trapping. Some of the dams built by the beaver still remain in some parts of this town. There was also an Indian path through this place, which connected the Delaware and Susquehanna rivers. It had the appearance of having been much travelled, and traces of it were distinctly seen and followed by some of the first settlers in this region.

Here these children of the forest tarried, and found their rich furs in trapping the beaver and the otter. Around these beautiful lakes, or natural ponds, whose waters are clear as crystal, and over these hills, the Indian boy found his sport in the chase for the deer and the elk. Here he drank and refreshed himself at these cool springs of water, and bathed in the limpid streams of his forest home. No white man molested him, or tempted him with the vices of civilization. As he pursued the plentiful game, or reposed in safety by these murmuring streams, and majestic rivers—he could say with a conscious independence. "This is my own" as well as "my native land."

III. SETTLEMENT.

But now another race of men has taken their places—a race more capable of developing the resources which the Creative Hand has here lodged. The entrance and work of the white man more particularly claim our attention.

The tract of land lying in the north part of this county, was bought of the aborigines, by Thomas and Richard Penn, heirs of William Penn, on the 5th of November, 1768. In this purchase was included a large portion of the State, extending diagonally from the northeast to the southwest corner. It was bought of the confederate tribes called the "Six Nations," in their general council, at Fort Stanvix—now the village of Rome, New York—for the sum of ten thousand dollars. Just six years after this event, that is to say in November 1774, a lot of land, upon which a part of this village stands, was bought of the proprietaries by one Christopher Hagar. This lot extended westward across the valley of the Lackawaxen to Belmont. It passed through several hands—purchasers who never intended to occupy it—when in June, 1789, it was purchased by Mr. Samuel Stanton, the first actual settler in this township. He was from Preston, New London County, Connecticut. Taking the route of New England emigration at that time, he proceeded up the Mohawk river. To gain the information he needed, with reference to wild lands, he came to Cooperstown, and had an interview with Mr. William Cooper, who was an agent for the sale of an extensive tract of wild land in this region. He soon engaged to accompany Mr. Cooper into this part of the State, and survey some land for him; having previously had some knowledge of this art. They proceeded down the Susquehanna, and leaving his family at Mr. Lane's, near Windsor, they entered this region. Here they were engaged some weeks in running out some lots of land upon the new road which had been constructed from the south part of the State. It was thought that this road would soon call in a large number of settlers. While thus engaged, he surveyed and purchased the lot of land as above mentioned. Having finished the intended surveys, they started homewards on the new road. They soon came to the camp of Mr. Samuel Preston, who, with Mr. John Hilborn, were then engaged in constructing this road. They had then encamped on or near the head waters of the Starucca Creek, about twelve miles from this village, and in the present township of Scott. Mr. Preston writes in his journal under date June 28, 1789, concerning his first interview with Mr. Stanton, thus: "While I was directing letters to send by John Hilborn, William Cooper came to my camp on his way to Otsego, as also his surveyor, Samuel Stanton. We moved to the camp by the spring, where I filled up for William Cooper several blank deeds, mortgages, &c." On the following day, Mr. Stanton signed, in this place, the deed for the above lot of land, containing 322 acres. For this he was to pay the sum of £322 to Thomas

Rogers, of Philadelphia, for whom, as proprietor, Mr. Cooper acted as agent.

It seems from a note in the first volume of the Town Records, in Mr. Stanton's handwriting, that on the next day he bought a large quantity of land in addition to the above lot. The note is as follows: "Samuel Stanton bought of William Cooper, agent for Thomas Franklin, William, and Andrew Craig, and others, nearly 3,000 acres on the 30th of June, 1789, and began to work on the land in June, 1790. Built a house and cleared some land."

After the business pertaining to this purchase was completed, Mr. Cooper left on the same day for Otsego, and Mr. Stanton remained in the employ of Mr. Preston. They soon finished this road to the State line—its proper terminus, according to the requisition of the "Act" which provided for its construction. He also aided Mr. Preston in constructing his own road down to the mouth of the Cascade Creek, on the Susquehanna river. Here Mr. Preston began a settlement which he supposed would eventually be a place of much business. During the summer he cleared several acres of land in this fertile valley; erected several dwelling houses; built a store, a blacksmith's shop, and a saw-mill. He named the place Harmony. Mr. Henry Drinker was associated with him in this enterprise; also Mr. John Hilborn, who afterwards made it the place of his future residence. Mr. Preston, however, superintended these improvements, and afterwards constructed a road connecting this place with the Delaware river, at

Stockport, where he subsequently settled and spent the remnant of his life. He supposed this road would be a great thoroughfare between the two rivers, while the north and south road would bring travel from the south, and both concentrate at Harmony.*

The next spring we find Mr. Stanton upon the lot of land he first purchased in this town, making improvements. He cleared a little land and built a small cabin.

A brief description of this cabin, in which the hardy pioneer of this town spent his first winter with his family, will not be out of place. Poor as it was, it was the best their circumstances would allow. It will also keep us reminded how many privations are endured by those enterprising men who have left the comforts of good society, to provide a home for their children, as well as to lay for them the foundations of good moral and religious institutions.

This cabin was situated a few rods southeast of Mr. Minor Mumford's residence. It was about ten rods east of the present Belmont and Easton Turnpike.

For the want of help to raise this cabin, it was built of poles. It was about twelve by fourteen feet on the ground, and had but one room. After he had raised it to such a height that he could stand upright in it, the poles were gradually drawn in on each side

* See Appendix, No. 6.

till they met at the ridge. Upon these were laid hemlock bark for a roof. A few stones were laid for a hearth, and built up a few feet in the rear, to form a protection against the fire. Upon this platform were piled huge logs, from which the smoke ascended and found its way out through an opening left in the roof for this purpose. The cabin stood with its ends east and west. The fire was at the east end. The door was in the south side. Windows it had none. He was able to bring but little household furniture into this wilderness. He, therefore, made use of such as he could hastily make with a few tools, from the native forest. There were no cabinet-makers—no saw-mills.

Mrs. Lillibridge, his daughter, in speaking of her parent's furniture when they first moved into this cabin, says: "It was not much. A white pine table, a chest of drawers with legs, two bedsteads which would now be worth about two dollars a-piece, four splint-bottom chairs, a trammel for the fire-place, a looking-glass, a few dishes set upon a shelf, pewter platters, pewter plates, and basins of the same materials; also some trenchers. Two children, a dog and a cat, made up the family circle when first they arrived in town." Mr. Stanton took slabs which he split from the logs, and constructed a door. Boards made in the same manner were used for the floor. Into this humble dwelling he moved his family on the tenth day of April, 1791. During this season he had the society of a few settlers, to be noticed hereafter, who had come without their families to begin improvements. They all left, however, in the autumn. He, with his family, remained alone in this vast wilderness to spend the winter. It proved to be a severe one. He had raised a scanty supply, which he hoped by proper care would be sufficient. The winter closed in with unusual rigor. His nearest neighbor lived about fourteen miles from him. The depth of the snow cut off all communications. A dense forest surrounded him. No friendly neighbor greeted him or inquired for his welfare. Not the sound of a human voice was heard, except those of his own family. With them he found his companions; with them he shared the wants and trials of the winter; with them the dreary nights and lingering months passed away. The storm rushed around his rude cabin, searching out its crevices, or rearing mimic Alps about his door.

But our solitary pioneer had other and more formidable difficulties to encounter. He was obliged to bring his hay, for two cows and a yoke of oxen, from a beaver meadow—a distance of nearly two miles. His wife in his absence, while attending on the duties of her household, had stepped upon the ice, slipped, and fractured a bone in her ancle. Privations and exposure brought on a severe cold: this was soon accompanied with a high fever. Soon her mind wandered, unconscious of her condition. The storm rushed around the poorly-covered cabin and sifted the snow upon her bed. Her youngest child, an infant of about five months old, also sickened. The father laid it at her side, but, alas! the delirious mother knew not her child. A raging fever had destroyed its natural aliment. His cows afforded no substitute for it. It rapidly declined under sickness and hunger. His stock of provisions were nearly exhausted. His potatoes had frozen by the unexpected severity of the winter. But even without this loss he would have had a scanty supply. He saw with regret that his provisions were not sufficient to supply even the limited wants of his family. Still, as they disappeared, he lived in hope that deliverance would come from some source ; yet no relief came. His wife still declined. That kind voice that had encouraged and cheered him in his toils in the wilderness, now uttered only incoherent sounds. Those active limbs, that had never tired in promoting the comfort of her loved companion and little ones, were now helpless. Those eyes, that had so long beamed with affection, now roamed about this scene of sorrow with a vacant stare. There were no kind neighbors near to call with some cooling draught for her fevered lips, and speak kind words of sympathy. He suffered alone in this vast wilderness. There were none to assist him or relieve him one moment in the care of his children and now more than helpless wife. No kind voice greeted him during these lonely and trying months—no hand brought relief. Obliged by these circumstances to remain at home, he saw hunger, famine, and perhaps death, coming upon himself and family with steady and relentless step. The snow had fallen to a great depth. Every path through these extensive forests was blocked up. Not a solitary wanderer attempted to penetrate it. True, indeed, the deer, the elk, the bear, and the panther roamed in these unbroken wilds ; but our pioneer was no hunter. He had no means of taking the animals that prowled around his dwelling. At length his food for his family was nearly exhausted. He had for several days kept his children on a small allowance, taking scarcely nothing himself. He still hoped that God would send relief. He divided his last provisions until they were reduced to a single meal. Before he distributed this, he hesitated. He looked over his beloved family, and his heart was moved. There, in the corner of the room, lay his sick wife, so wasted under disease and want that the light of reason had become extinguished. By her side lay an infant child, pining away for the want of the aliment suited to its years. On either side of him were his two little children, looking up to him with tearful eyes for bread. He arose and took the last morsel and divided it between them. It was a trying hour. Without speedy relief those helpless children must cry in vain for bread. A lingering, dreadful death awaited them. Painful thought! Must I see these loved ones pine away with hunger ? Must I hear their unavailing cry for food ? Must I close their eyes in death, and here, alone, bury their wasted forms in the wilderness ? O, how can a father's heart bear all this ? Such thoughts, as we may well imagine, led him with unusual earnestness to Him " who provideth for the raven his food." He there kneeled before God, with his family, and committed them to Him, hoping and trusting in His mercy for deliverance. He arose from prayer and went to his door, when he heard a dog bark upon the opposite hill, near where this village now stands. He distinctly heard the dog as if closely chasing an animal down the hill to the Lackawaxen. Elated with the hope of deliverance, he seized an old musket which had long been useless, and ran down to the stream, where he found an elk in the water, defending himself from the dog. So intense were the emotions of that hour, that without reflection he repeatedly snapped the old musket, but of course to no effect. The hunter, whose dog had roused the elk, soon came down the hill and shot it. He, with his companion, who had come out on snow shoes for a hunt, soon learned the condition of Mr. Stanton and his family. They immediately emptied their knapsacks of palatable food for them. They roasted a part of the elk, and before its flesh was yet fully cooked, Mr. Stanton, as a starving man, eagerly devoured it. After relieving their immediate wants, they went to obtain other comforts for this afflicted family in the wilderness. Mr. Stanton was soon visited by his cousin, Mr. Asa Stanton, who had recently settled near Weymart. To these visits, and the frequent visits of these hunters, he was indebted for many comforts, and the restoration of his wife and infant child to health. The hunter who found Mr. Stanton in this distressed situation was Mr. Frederic Coates. Mr. Stanton ever after regarded this visit, and very justly too, as a remarkable interposition of Divine Providence. He preserved the horns of this elk as a momento of God's mercy to him and his family while in a sick and starving condition. Some years afterwards he kept a public house and had them nailed upon the top of his sign-post, and often related to visitors and travellers the story of his suffering and deliverance.

It will not be out of place here to give a more extended account of this man, who was first in this town to meet the difficulties of a settlement in the wilderness. In his physical aspect he was heavy-built, tall, broad-shouldered, but not corpulent. He had a light complexion, soft blue eye, very light brown hair, with whiskers verging a little to the sandy shade. He was always sanguine in whatever enterprise he undertook. His imagination was lively, and would picture before him the result before he had properly weighed the difficulties to be encountered. In his deportment and common habits he had no refinement. His person and things around him indicated great neglect. His intellectual faculties were, however, well developed. He had a great desire for the acquisition of knowledge. If not occupied with company, or other pressing duties, he might be found with some book in his hand. Those who saw him most, usually found him, if alone, sitting in his bar-room, with his feet perched upon some object higher than his head, absorbed in reading. At such times he seemed not to care how affairs went around him. His cows might be in his garden, or his wife destitute of wood, or his bar-room unswept and in total disorder : he would sit for hours absorbed in reading. Nor was this any dreamy mood. His mind grasped and retained with an unusual memory whatever he read. One who was intimately acquainted with him has informed me that he had read more than two thousand volumes, and could converse intelligently about the contents of each one of them.

He also had a sociable nature. In conversation he was free, affable, entertaining, and serious, rather than jovial. He was extremely inquisitive, and had a happy faculty of becoming acquainted with strangers who put up with him. He had also an easy way of entertaining them with a great variety of anecdotes. He was not easily forgotten by those who had once stopped at his tavern. It was his natural turn to be engaged in matters of public interest and improvement. He took a prominent part in securing the "act" for the "Cochecton and Great Bend Turnpike." This was *then* considered a greater achievement than the construction of a canal or a railroad would *now* be. He possessed a good judgment, and was considered a safe adviser in matters of a legal and public nature. He was appointed Justice of the Peace in 1796, while this region belonged to Northampton County. When this county was organized in 1798, he was appointed one of the commissioners to locate the Seat of Justice, and erect the courthouse and jail. In a vote taken on this question, he found himself alone in favor of a more northern location. After much argument, he, for the sake of unanimity, voted with the others. This gave offence to this part of the county, which he represented. He soon published a pamphlet, in which he advocated his opinion, and attempted to justify the course he had taken. Whatever may be thought of his course in casting his vote against his better judgment, it is worthy of note, as an honor to his good judgment, that within three years the seat of Justice was removed northward to Bethany. In October, 1814, he was appointed associate-judge in this county. He held this office until he left this part of the State.

We have never discovered but a single instance in which his good judgment failed him. This was in conceiving himself to be a poet. But, if he erred here, he has but followed the track of many a great and good man before him. We find recorded upon the town book some rhymes in his own handwriting. They so intimately relate to the early history of this township, that they cannot well be omitted in this discourse. They are entitled, "The Golden Age of Mount Pleasant, from 1791 to 1796, while eighty-two miles from Easton, the seat of justice. There was no law put in force but the law of forbearance. Having no law, the people were a law unto themselves." So runs the title.

But it may be well here to state the history of the origin of these verses, that you may be better able to appreciate their sentiments. Mr. Stanton conceived the idea that the people of this new and isolated country ought to have an Almanac suited to their times and circumstances. He, therefore, made a proposition to Judge Samuel Preston, of Stockport, who was quite a mathematician, to do the figuring, and he would write the poetry usually placed at the head of the page. He, therefore, went to work, and the following verses are the result:

1. "Secluded here from noise and strife,
   We lead a quiet, peaceful life.
   No loungers here with poisonous breath,
   Nor doctors here to deal out death.

2. No trainings here, nor such like trash,
   To waste our time and spend our cash ;
   Nor town meetings to choose our masters,
   To make us slaves and breed disasters.

3. No priest sends round his man for pay,
   Because that he did preach and pray ;
   For we believe that grace is free
   To all who wish to taste and see.

4. No jockey merchants here prevail,
   To trust their goods, then send to jail ;
   Nor fiddling strolling players dare
   Infest the place, our youth to snare.

5. Some slaves to *forms* may now inquire,
   Have you no court-house, jail, or Squire ?
   While all are honest and sincere,
   What need of court or prison here ?

6. Have we a cause to settle ? then
   We leave it to judicious men
   To search the matter well, and we
   To their just judgments do agree.

7. The noise of war, or the excise,
   Does neither vex our ears nor eyes ;
   For we are free from every tax,
   And stay at home and swing the ax.

8. Our corn we pound, our wheat we boil,
   Thus eat the product of our soil.
   Sweet Independence here does reign,
   And we've no reason to complain.

9. Yet we, like others, still look on
Till we shall get our mill to run;
Then we'll not pound and boil again,
But live in *style* like other men.

10. From sheep we make our clothing warm,
In·which we face the wintry storm;
They likewise give us meat and light,
To feast by day and see by night.

11. Do we want wild meat? then we kill
Elk, deer, or bear, and eat our fill.
Sometimes we've fowl and sometimes fish,
But rarely meet an empty dish.

12. Here healing herbs and roots do grow,
And sugar-juice from maples flow.
Molasses, vinegar, and beer,
Are made from sugar orchards here.

13. Sometimes we live on pork and peas,
Then milk and honey, butter, cheese—
Plain food and exercise agree
To make us happy while we're free."

We will add, that Judge Preston never completed the mathematics: so that this New World was never benefited by the almanac. But it is just to say that *such* poetry was not without its benefit. It was published in some periodical, and read by one John Bunting, a Quaker in New Jersey, and a man highly respected, who was so pleased with the description of things, that he soon moved into this region. His descendants are now in this county.

As a Christian man, Mr. Stanton is uniformly spoken of in commendable terms. In this respect, his memory is blessed. He has left the savor of godliness behind him. His religious poetry is of a more elevated character. I have been able to find but one piece: this is entitled, "The Complainer

Reformed," and is written as though it was his own experience. This hymn consists of twelve verses, and was considered worthy a place in a collection of religious hymns used by the Free Communion Baptist Church.* It may be found on the 185th page of that book, which has been furnished me by Mr. Luther Starks. His religious views, while they were strictly evangelical on all the doctrines of grace, were of a liberal character. He fellowshipped Christians of all evangelical denominations. As early as 1797, he cordially welcomed the Rev. Daniel Thatcher, a missionary of the General Assembly of the Presbyterian Church, to preach in his house. At this service he invited Christians of all denominations to meet, and there, for the first time in this place, the Sacrament of the Lord's Supper was administered to nine professed disciples scattered in this wilderness. It was a memorable event. He was always ready to open his house for religious meetings. His shed and barn were, for several years, the usual place for holding the yearly meetings of the Free Communion Baptist Church. He had painted upon his sign the following, as he thought, appropriate passage of Scripture : " Be not forgetful to entertain strangers." This, surmounted as it was by the horns of an elk, would naturally remind a hungry, weary traveller through this wilderness, of a scriptural tavern keeper, with a good liberal steak of venison. Few taverns at the present day awaken similar associations.

* Since writing the above, the author has been furnished with a manuscript, containing about fifty hymns, which breathe the spirit of true devotion.

Mr. Stanton, near the close of his life, removed from this town to reside in the western part of this State. He had been appointed a commissioner of a State road in that section. Having business, growing out of this office, to transact in Harrisburg, he took his family down to the west branch of the Susquehanna, where he left them to proceed on their way, while he went to Harrisburg. Having completed the object of his visit there, he directed his course to meet his family. He came to Bellefonte, in Centre County, and stopped with his friend Judge Burnside, where he was taken sick. Every effort was made to restore health, but he rapidly declined, and, after a few days' illness, ended his mortal life, April 15th, 1816.

IV. ORDER OF SETTLEMENTS.

The order of time in which the first settlers came into this town is as follows: Mr. Stanton made his first purchase as a settler in this township, on the 29th of June, 1789. We may, therefore, fix the first settlement of this town at this date, which will be sixty-seven years ago next June. In the spring of 1790, having brought his family down the river, he left them at Mr. Lane's near Windsor, and came into this town, and worked upon the lot he had just purchased. He built his cabin and cleared a few acres.

On the next spring he moved his family, consisting of his wife and two children, the oldest of whom was nearly four years of age. He occupied the cabin he had built the year before. Mr. Silas Kellogg also came in with him to begin a settlement. He brought with him two hired men. This company came from Harmony with ox-teams and sleds, upon which they brought their goods and farming implements, besides the family. They were four days on their way—a distance of 28 miles. The road, though having been once cut through, had become much obstructed. They arrived here on the 10th day of April, 1791. Mr. Kellogg had emigrated from Ballstown, Saratoga County, New York. It had been his intention to settle in Western New York; but from representations made to him of the anticipated growth of this region, he directed his course hither. His brother, Mr. Eliphalet Kellogg, who had not yet visited this region, had purchased a lot of land in this township on the 9th of August, 1790. This lot was transferred to Mr. Silas Kellogg on the 2d of Feb., 1791. He settled on this lot, and made his first clearing on the bank of the Lackawaxen. In that beautiful opening of this valley which lies immediately below Mr. Heman J. Wheeler's residence, he, with his two hired men, began their summer's work. During the season they cleared and sowed to wheat fourteen acres of land. Mr. Kellogg has been heard to say that, in order to procure the seed, he was obliged to go with his ox-team to Harmony—then a distance of twenty-eight miles—and thence down the river to Great Bend. It was a journey of nearly two weeks. Having accomplished his work, he returned to Ballstown to spend the winter. During this season, also, Mr.

Elijah Dix and his son, a boy of eleven years old, came, and began to work a lot of land he had purchased. He was from Williamstown, Massachusetts. He built a log house a few rods east of Mr. E. Richardson's late residence, where, also, he began his first improvement. There were in all nine residents of this town during the summer of 1791. Concerning this year, Mr. Stanton has written in the town book as follows: " This summer, at any heavy work, such as raising log-houses, we were able to raise six hands. And, considering ourselves so strong, we undertook opening a road toward the Great Bend, some south of where the turnpike road was made afterward."

At the close of the summer, all but Mr. Stanton and his family left for the winter. The sufferings he endured here while shut out from human society, have already been related.

1792. As the next spring opened, Mr. Kellogg returned. He was at this time but twenty-four years of age. He was still unmarried, and had drank deeply of the spirit of western emigration. He possessed a good constitution, and had an intelligent, active mind. He was ambitious and ardent in his expectation of securing great results in this his first enterprise. He laid out extensive plans, and entered upon them with a firm expectation of success. He purchased a tract of about three thousand acres of land in this township, and made it his residence for life. He died at the residence of his son, Mr. Jerry Kellogg, on the 15th of August, 1853, at the advanced age of 86 years.

About the last of February, Mr. John Tiffany, from

Attlebury, Massachusetts, stopped at this place on his way to the Nine Partners. He had his wife and three children with him. While tarrying, he concluded to remain here and make it his home. He purchased the farm now owned by Mr. Chistopher, built first a log-house, and then the house now occupied on that place. On the 5th day of March, Mr. Joseph Stearns and Mr. Jirah Mumford arrived, who also were on their way to the Nine Partners. They were from Tolland County, Connecticut. They had put their teams together, making two yoke of oxen attached to a sled. They were three weeks on their way. Mr. Stearns had his two sons, James and Otis, with him, and also a hired man. He found on his arrival that the provisions of the settlers were far too limited for such an increased company. He, therefore, left immediately for Great Bend, and procured two bushels of cornmeal. He then went to the Nine Partners, where he had spent the previous summer. Mr. Mumford, however, concluded to remain. He had brought with him his son Thomas, then a boy of twelve years old, and *still* living in this town, and also two hired men. He purchased two hundred acres of land, and built a log-house near where his son Minor now lives. In the fall, he returned with his son to Connecticut, and spent the winter. Mr. Stearns, near the close of the season, went to Connecticut, and brought in his family, which then included eight children. Having arrived at this place, the people of the Nine Partners came to aid him through to that place. But he concluded to relinquish his improvements there, and make a home in this settlement. He lived during the winter in the house Mr. Mumford had built.

Mr. Dix also returned in the spring of this year, and occupied the log-house which he had built the previous summer. He brought with him a family of eight children. He had formerly been a man of some wealth, but had lost most of it by the depreciation of Continental money. He came into this new county to retrieve his loss, and provide a future home for his family. The second winter, therefore, found four families here, besides Mr. Kellogg, to share each other's wants and trials, and form a society for social and religious enjoyment.

1793. As the spring opened, Mr. Jirah Mumford returned with his family, consisting of four children. He occupied the house he had built the previous summer. Mr. Stearns, who had lived in it during the winter, removed to Mr. Elijah Dix's house. He (Mr. Stearns) had purchased the farm now owned by Mr. Noah Chittenden. During the summer he built his house nearly opposite Mr. Asa Smith's residence.

Mr. Joseph Tanner also moved into the settlement this spring, from Preston, Connecticut. He had but one child. His purchase included a greater part of this village, but lying mostly north of it. He built his house nearly half a mile north of this village, by the side of a large spring, where the main road east and west, *now* running through *this village*, was originally constructed.

We also notice a Mr. Amasa Geer, as a settler this

year. He built a house by a noted spring, as you descend the hill westward, on land now owned by Mr. T. H. Brown. Mr. Jacobus Barrager also moved into the settlement this year. These two individuals, however, remained but a few years.

During the last week in May of this year, a young man not twenty years old entered this settlement, from the West. He had a small bundle which he carried in one hand, and with the other he used a staff. He was weary, penniless and alone. He had left his home in New England, on the sixth of the same month, with $11 75 in his pocket, to become acquainted with the resources of the vast territories of our country then unoccupied. He had started out on life's errand with a determination to construct his own fortune, and establish his own character. Nature had endowed him with an active, well-balanced mind, and a vigorous constitution. He had early been taught, and heartily received the great moral and religious principles which constitute the best foundation for success. He had a fixed and unalterable purpose in carrying them out in the duties and conflicts of life. His name was Jason Torrey. He had come from Williamstown, Massachusetts, his native place, on foot. He had crossed the Hudson near Kinderhook, passed through Harpersfield, in Delaware County, and reached the Susquehanna, near Unadilla. He followed this river down to Great Bend, and from thence to this place. Arriving here, he stopped at the house of Mr. Elijah Dix, with whom he had previously been acquainted. In June 27, we find him at work with his ax, when Mr. Baird, of Pottstown, near Philadelphia, came and engaged him to survey some land on the Lackawaxen, for him. Again in July, while in the employment of Mr. Jirah Mumford, who released him from an engagement to work for him, he left on a surveying tour for the same man, through different parts of this region of the State. On his return he resumed his engagement with Mr. Mumford, and worked till the 18th of October, when he started on his return to Williamstown. To secure the great object for which he had left home, he took a circuitous route. He followed the Susquehanna from Great Bend to Owego, from thence he went to the Cayuga Lake, then taking the Genessee road he passed through Oneida and Whitesboro, and then down the Mohawk through Albany to Williamstown, making a distance travelled since he left home, of 900 miles, most of which he had performed on foot.

In the next spring, 1794, he left with the same object in view. He went to Philadelphia, and from thence came to this place, and then proceeded westward as far as Lake Ontario. Again, in December, 1795, he went to Philadelphia, in which city and vicinity he remained until July, when after some hesitation whether to settle in Pennsylvania or Western New York, he decided upon the former.

He then proceeded up through Pottstown and Nazareth, slept in the woods one night near Blooming Grove, then followed up the Lackawaxen through where Honesdale now stands, to this place. He engaged to Mr. Mumford again, in mowing, that he might, as he says, "harden his hands for chopping." He had deliberately made up his mind, after exploring the best portions of New York and Pennsylvania, here to settle and spend his life. He had seen more promising fields for wealth, but he regarded the character of the society in which he was to live and educate his family as of more importance than the rapid increase of riches. With such principles he could pass over the most fertile soil and locate upon these hills.

The result has confirmed his wisdom. The difficulties he here met in the early settlement of this county, developed those sterling qualities of mind and heart which have made him a distinguished and useful man. In his first effort he encountered difficulties which would have *disheartened* many persons. But when once his mind was fixed upon any object to be accomplished, nothing but absolute impossibilities deterred him. He had designed to encamp upon the land which he had purchased in the eastern part of this town, and commence clearing the land, but no pork could be obtained in the settlement. This being a necessary article in this work, he went to Blooming Grove, bought nineteen pounds, at one shilling per pound, and some salt, at the rate of $3 per bushel, and returned with them upon his back. But now, when ready to enter upon his enterprise, he was afflicted with a severe sickness. He was confined for five weeks at the residence of Mr. Elijah Dix, part of the time helpless, and apparently nigh unto death. When he had sufficiently recovered he returned home. Still fixed upon his purpose, we find him (March 16th, 1797) again starting for Stantonville, as this settlement was then called. At this time he came with a horse, by the way of Esopus and Cochecton. During this summer his brother Samuel was with him. He built a log-house, and made improvements on his farm. He was also, during the season, interested in the construction of a new road from this village to Minisink. It is the present turnpike road connecting this place with Bethany, and proceeding from thence to its intersection with the Milford and Owego turnpike. He selected the route, and assisted in cutting out the trees, more or less, with his own ax.

In the December following he went to Williamstown, and returned with his wife, whom he had married in January preceding. They came, bringing all their goods and furniture in the same sleigh in which they rode. They arrived at the log-house, and entered it on the 11th day of February, 1798. Here he resided until he removed to the county seat. He had two sons born in this house—William and Ephraim. The latter died at the age of twenty-four.

In 1801 Mr. Torrey surveyed and set the stakes for the public square and Court-house, in the present village of Bethany. It had been selected as the place where the County-seat should be located. But at that time not a foot of land had been cleared, nor a tree cut within two miles of it. He immediately commenced building a dwelling-house. "The old family mansion was the first house erected; and while building this house, he travelled daily from Mount Pleasant and back, twelve miles, through a wilderness, to carry his workmen their provisions. The first court held there was organized in the old homestead. The upper rooms were unfinished, and chairs were set on a joiner's bench for the judges, while the jury occupied seats below. Then, and for years afterwards, Mr. Torrey was personally acquainted with every family in the county, and was well informed of all their circumstances. The purchases of real estate by new settlers were, to a very large extent, made through his agency. In the year 1818, the church at Bethany was organized, and then Mr. Torrey made a profession of religion, and was soon after elected a ruling Elder. At the time of his death, he was the oldest-ordained Elder in any Church in the northern part of this State."*

He entered heartily into all the efforts made to plant the institutions of the Gospel in this new county. He was a liberal supporter of the Gospel in the church of which he was a member. Though a change of the County-seat led to the removal of his residence to Honesdale, three miles distant, he never removed his church relation. He still contributed as before to the church which he had aided in its infancy, and which now had been weakened by removals. In his will, he made provision for a like sum to be paid annually from his estate, during a term of years, for the

* Funeral Discourse of Jason Torrey, by Henry A. Rowland, D. D.

support of the Gospel in that Church. All evangelical clergymen traversing the dense forests, to reach the scattered population of this county, and break unto them the bread of life, were sure to meet at his door a cordial welcome. Here they and their horses have been often refreshed on their way. In him they found a generous and sympathizing friend.

Through a train of providential events "Mr. Torrey had become owner of a large tract of land, about three miles south of Bethany, where the canal of the Delaware and Hudson Canal Company terminates; and on this spot the borough of Honesdale is now located. The first settlement was begun in 1826. The first house was erected by Mr. Torrey, at the forks of the Dyberry and West branch of the Lackawaxen, and was afterwards converted into a Church, and designated as the Old Tabernacle."*

Here he resided to the close of his life. He had the pleasure of seeing a beautiful village of some 3,000 inhabitants spring into existence, while over the extensive fields of his early surveys, where the wild beasts had roamed unmolested, he witnessed with equal satisfaction beautiful farms, church edifices, mills of various kinds, and villages, with the various blessings of a thriving and virtuous society. Admonished by the approaching infirmities of age that the day of life was drawing to a close, he made liberal bequests to the cause of Christ, and retired from active business—then leaning upon his Almighty Sav-

* Funeral discourse, &c.

iour, quietly and peacefully descended to the grave.

We proceed to notice but one more settler in this town during this year. Mr. Jacob Van Meter came to this place, on his way from Salem County, New Jersey, to Western New York. He was here overtaken by the autumnal storms, and concluded to settle in this township. He had a family of five children. Soon after he purchased and built the place where his son Charles now lives. He spent the remnant of his life in this town.

1795. This year Mr. John S. Rogers, from New Jersey, a Quaker, purchased and settled with his family. He had eight children. He built about one mile east of Mr. Joseph Peck's residence. Here he passed the remainder of his days.

Mr. Joseph Stevenson, from New Jersey, also came this year. He purchased a farm in the vicinity of the octagon stone school-house. He had six children, the oldest of whom was over twenty-one years of age. We also notice Mr. Seymore Allen, who came this year, and bought Geer's farm and improvement. He soon after sold it to Mr. Ichabod Starks, who continued to occupy it for many years, and there closed his earthly days.

Mr. Abram Cramer also settled here this year. He bought a place, and built a little south of Mr. Thomas Slayton's residence, where there is now a house made of hewn logs. He had a family of eight children. He died in this township.

This year Mr. Elijah Peck moved his family into

this settlement. He had emigrated from Connecticut, and came to this place by way of Cooperstown. He had previously been here, purchased the farm where his widow now lives, made some improvement, and built a log-house on an old road which was constructed north of the present turnpike. He had then a family of three children. He subsequently became a minister in the Baptist Church, as we shall have occasion to notice. He died in this town at an advanced age.

This year Mr. Jirah Mumford completed a grist-mill and a saw-mill. This was considered a great acquisition to this new settlement. They were located near where Mr. Edward M. Atwater now has a saw-mill. The grist-mill was about twenty feet square. It had one run of stones, which were about three feet in diameter. It had one bolt about seven feet long. The meal was taken by hand and poured into the bolt, which the miller turned with a crank. The saw-mill, by diligent use, and a full head of water, would saw about 700 feet per day. Yet these were the only mills within twenty-five or thirty miles, and they were often rendered useless in the winter season.

1796. This year Mr. Benjamin King came to this place from the Paupack settlement. He was then a young, unmarried man, and purchased the farm now owned by Mr. George Moase. He built the house and barn now standing upon the place, and occupied the farm about twenty years. He is still living in this vicinity, at an advanced age.

His brother, Mr. Charles King, came at the same time, and a few years after bought and cultivated a farm, east of the late Benjamin Wheeler's residence.

This year, also, Mr. Samuel Meredith, a man of wealth in Philadelphia, began to make improvements in this town. He first built an ashery, for making pot and pearlash. This enterprise, however, failed. He had invested a large part of his fortune in a tract of land in this region. Not finding as ready sale for this land as he expected, he retired from the city, and built in the west part of this town a well-finished house, at a cost of about six thousand dollars. He named the place of his residence Belmont, which name it has retained to this day.

His father, whose name was Reese Meredith, settled in Philadelphia at an early day. He was from England, and a Welshman by birth. In his own country he was a man of rank and wealth. He warmly espoused the cause of the American Colonies. His first interview with General Washington was when he held the office of Colonel in the Virginia troops. He at once formed a high opinion of him, and was ever after his firm and intimate friend. In the most trying period of the war, when the faith of many wavered, he boldly encouraged its prosecution. When the army were suffering for food and clothing, he promptly came to their relief, and freely contributed the sum of five thousand pounds sterling. At the close of the war, when Washington was called to the Presidential chair, he promoted his son, Samuel Meredith, to the office of Treasurer of the United States.

The following letters, the original copies of which are now in the hands of the family, will show the estimation in which he was held, as well as the term of his office.

The first is from Alexander Hamilton, the Secretary of the Treasury. It is as follows:

TREASURY OFFICE, NEW YORK,
September 13, 1789.

SIR :—Permit me to congratulate you on your appointment as Treasurer of the United States, and to assure you of the pleasure I feel in anticipating your coöperation with me in a station in which a character like yours is so truly valuable.

I need not observe to you how important it is that you should be on the ground as soon as possible. The call for your presence, you will be sensible, is urgent. Mr. Duer, my assistant, goes to Philadelphia to procure a loan from the Bank there. He will communicate with you, and, I am persuaded, will meet with your concurrence in whatever may facilitate the object of his mission.

With sincere esteem

I am, Sir,

Your obedient servant,

ALEXANDER HAMILTON,
Secretary of the Treasury.

SAMUEL MEREDITH, Esq.,
Treasurer of the United States.

Mr. Meredith entered upon the duties of this office when the Treasury was in its most embarrassed and confused state. He resigned it in 1801.

The following letter from Thomas Jefferson, then President of the United States, shows the fidelity and ability with which he had *fulfilled* the duties of this office :

MONTICELLO, *September* 4, 1801.

DEAR SIR :—I received yesterday your favor of August 29, resigning your office of Treasurer of the United States, after the last of October next. I am sorry for the circumstances which dictate the measure to you ; but from their nature, and the deliberate consideration of which it seems to be the result, I presume that dissuasives on my part would be without effect. My time in office has not been such as to bring me into an intimate insight of the proceedings of the several departments, but I am sure I hazard nothing when I testify in your favor—that you have conducted yourself with perfect integrity and propriety in the duties of the office you have filled, and I pray you to be assured of my high esteem and consideration.

THOMAS JEFFERSON.

MR. MEREDITH.

Soon after Mr. Meredith closed the duties of this office, he commenced his residence in this town, and retired from public life. Having spent the remnant of his days here, he departed this life February 10, 1817, in the 76th year of his age.

His remains lie in the family cemetery, by the side of Mrs. Meredith's, his accomplished wife. His tomb rests upon one of the gentle declivities of the Moosic mountain, and overlooks the beautiful valley of the Lackawaxen.

It seems that this settlement had now attracted attention at the Capitol, and Mr. Samuel Stanton was this year appointed by the Governor, Thomas Mifflin, Justice of the Peace for this region, then belonging to Northampton County. This was the first appointment of a Justice of the Peace north of Stroudsburg.

We are not able to relate in detail, the order and names of the settlers who subsequently came into this town. I will, however, remark, that the current of emigration, until about the year 1820, or 1825, was chiefly from New England. New England people have, from the first settlement, exerted a preponderating influence in giving character to society. It still retains, to a great degree, those early impressions. At a very early period of the settlement, Mr. Tench Cox, a landholder from Philadelphia, spent a few days here, and afterwards remarked, as a matter of curiosity, that the people in Stantonville would lay aside their work at sundown on Saturday night, and begin the Sabbath. Then, on Sunday evening, the women would take their knitting-work. He had never seen the custom before. This is strictly a New England custom. The attachments of this people to their Puritan ancestors may be seen, from the cherished relics brought from New England. Among these we notice a trammel and a sea-chest, which were brought over in the Mayflower. They have descended in the line of the Brewster family, and are owned by Mr. Calvally Freeman, a descendant of that family. There is also an ancient book, entitled "Christ the Way and the Truth and the Life." On the title-page, its authorship is thus described: "Written by the eminently Pious, Godly, and Zealous Mr. John Brown, Minister of the Gospel at Wamphray, in Annandale, in the time of his banishment in Holland." "Printed at Glasgow, by Alexander Miller, 1738." This was undoubtedly written more than fifty years previous to this date, inasmuch as the persecution which led to the banishment of a large number of the dissenting clergymen of Scotland, terminated in 1690. The book was brought here at an early day by Mr. James Bigelow, and now owned by his son, Mr. James H. Bigelow. He also has a copy of "The Confession of Faith of the General Assembly of the Presbyterian Church," containing also "The Sum of Saving Knowledge," "The First National Covenant of Scotland," "The Solemn League and Covenant," and "The Directory for the Publick Worship of God." Printed in Glasgow, 1749. These books, with others of a similar nature, were the chosen companions of his father, Mr. James Bigelow, while here in this new country.

V. FIRST THINGS.

There are some events and items of interest bearing upon the history of this town, which take their interest only from the fact of their *priority.* Among these I notice that the first child born in this township was born August 26, 1791. She was a daughter of Mr. Samuel Stanton. She married Mr. Thomas Lillibridge, and now lives in the State of Illinois.

The first male child was born June 18, 1793. His name is Jabez Stearns. He now lives in the town of Lebanon, in this county.

The first wedding in this town took place January 1, 1796. The parties were Mr. Silas Kellogg and the eldest daughter of Mr. Jirah Mumford. There were at that time no magistrates here—no resident clergymen. They were obliged to send to the Delaware river for the Rev. Ezekiel Sampson, a Baptist clergyman, who came twenty miles through the wilderness, by marked trees, and duly united in matrimony the first wedded couple in this township. One who was present at that wedding, and now living, says, that nearly every man, woman, and child in the town were present, and all accommodated in one room.

The first adult person that died in this town was Mr. Jacob Van Meter, the eldest son of Jacob Van Meter, senior. He died in the fall of 1796. Previous to this, a child of two or three years old had died. It belonged to Zebulon Tanner, who resided temporarily here as a chopper for the settlers.

The first frame building was a barn, built by Mr. Silas Kellogg, in 1794. It stood nearly opposite the residence of Mr. Charles Kennedy. The first framed dwelling-house was built the next year by Mr. Joseph

Tanner. It was situated north of the village, by a cluster of apple-trees, still remaining. The road from the east passed through there before the turnpike was constructed. Here the first store in town was opened under the firm of " Granger & Tanner," in 1806. It was the only store within twenty miles. Their annual trade amounted to $3,000.

There was no building in this village until the "Cochecton and Great Bend Turnpike" was constructed. The first house was built by Mr. Joseph Tanner in 1808, a few feet west of Mr. George Soper's residence. He used it as a dwelling, a store, and an office in which to transact his business as Justice of the Peace. He also built a tavern two stories high, a few feet east of it. These were burnt in 1811.

The first Justice of the Peace after the organization of this town and county, was Mr. Joseph Tanner. Mr. Stanton having been commissioned to act in Northampton County, no longer held this office. The first Constable was Benjamin Dix. Joseph Tanner and Elijah Peck were the first Supervisors of this town.

VI. TRIALS AND SUFFERINGS OF THE SETTLERS.

The privations and sufferings endured by persons who have penetrated into the wilderness and made it a home, are themes often dwelt upon with interest. We should never forget the sacrifices made by our fathers, to procure for us a comfortable home. We have already related some of them—all can never be be told. Still, justice demands that something more on this point should be said. These sufferings arose from their secluded position and the incipient stage of everything.* One of the greatest difficulties was the want of a sufficient quantity of grain, and suitable means of preparing it for food. Many of the early settlers boiled their grain; others hollowed out a stump, and with a large pestle, attached to a bent sapling, pounded it. One man in town dressed out two stones of about two feet in diameter, in the shape of mill-stones. Having adjusted the upper one on a pivot, one turned it with a crank, while another threw in a handful of grain as fast as it was ground.

Mr. Silas Kellogg says he has brought in provisions from Great Bend upon his back; and that in climbing the hills beneath his heavy burden, his vision has become double, so that he was obliged to sit down till his regular sight was restored.

Mr. Benjamin King says, that soon after he came here, he went with an ox-team four miles above Chenango Forks, to buy grain. He broke his road through a deep snow. There were then but three or four settlers between here and the Great Bend. It was a journey of more than ten days. The mills being frozen in that region, he was obliged, on his return, to make another journey to Waullenpaupach, to get it ground. He has frequently been to Wilkesbarre on horse-back, with maple sugar, and exchanged it for grain—returning with four and a half bushels upon his horse.

* See Appendix, No. 7.

On another occasion of destitution, Mr. Jason Torrey took his oxen to the Delaware river, sold them, and with the money went to Stroudsburg, procured a horse, and brought home a load of flour. He travelled in this journey about eighty miles. Having reached home, he first distributed a portion among his neighbors before eating any himself, that all might rejoice together.

Mrs. Lillibridge, daughter of Mr. Stanton, says that on one occasion, a poor neighbor who had a large family, and in a destitute state, called to borrow some flour of her father. He promised to pay it when he could go some thirty miles, earn it, and bring it home on his back. Mr. Stanton had but a half bushel of flour in his house. But he divided it, and gave him half, saying: "There will be some way provided; we shall not starve." That night a man came along, on his way to New York, with a load of flour. He stopped over night at Mr. Stanton's house. He urged him to sell him a barrel, but he positively refused. The next morning one of his horses was very lame, so that he was obliged to leave the entire load for sale. Mr. Stanton ever spoke of it as an overruling Providence.

Mr. Joseph Stearns had a family of eight children. On one occasion he was so reduced for food, that he went to Great Bend, and purchased two bushels of wheat, had it ground, and brought it home on his back. At another time he was destitute of meat, which was greatly needed, to endure the hard work required to lay the forest. Weakened by such toil, he was much cast down at his lot here in the wilderness. His wife, however, who was a devotedly pious woman, endeavored to encourage him by referring to that overruling Providence which had directed them here, and would still provide. Her confidence increasing as she dwelt upon this subject, she arose and said to her husband : "Now, I will hang the pot over the fire, and I believe the Lord will fill it." Her confidence was not mistaken, for before the water boiled a fawn, apparently frightened, entered the field where her boys were at work. They chased it a few rods, and easily captured it in a thicket of bushes, where Mr. Asa Smith's tannery now stands. As they joyfully entered the cabin door, the father remembered the words of encouragement and faith so recently spoken, and resolved no more to distrust God. On another occasion this good woman, when her husband and older sons had gone to their work, went out to the woods where they had been making sugar, to save some sap that was wasting. Having no one with whom to leave her infant child, she took it with her. She made a cradle of a sap-trough, and laid him down by the side of a large log. While busy here and there gathering the sap, she looked towards the child, and saw an enormous bear upon the log, looking down into his innocent face, and in the very act of grabbing him in his extended jaws. She uttered a wild shriek of terror and fell exhausted. The old dog saw the peril of the child and instantly flew to his rescue. That child is now Mr. Ashbel Stearns, who still lives in this vicinity. Not long after this, she had been over to Mr. Stanton's, on a visit with this same infant, having her son Otis, then a young lad, with her. While on their return, as they were in a footpath, crossing a rivulet in the rear of the present dwelling of Mr. Jonathan Miller, sen., a large bear came out of the brush and stood directly before them. Her son was at the time carrying the infant. But that faithful dog, that had once saved his life, came up and rushed upon the bear, who speedily retreated.

In an early period of this settlement, Mrs. Mumford had suffered her two little girls, Deborah and Sally, to go home with a near neighbor. One was about four and the other about six years old. They were returning by a foot-path, and mistaking the right direction, wandered off into the wilderness. They had been gone some hours before it was discovered that they were lost. The whole town roused in the search; but the night closed in and no trace could be found of them. No efforts were spared with lanterns and torches throughout the night, but all in vain. The next day people came from a great distance, and the woods were searched, but no children could be found. The second night spread its dark curtain over the distracted family. The heart-broken mother wrung her hands in agony. She would take her little infant, that clung to her breast with a tremulous fear, and go out at the midnight hour, and lie upon the cold ground, exclaiming, " Is this all the bed my dear little ones have to-night!" She would know *herself* how cold and damp it was. Thus the second night of agony passed. As the morning dawned, the fond mother bent under the crushing conflict of hope and fear. Yet hope was still strong that she should again see her dear children alive. Every man met for consultation and concert of action. They separated themselves within hearing distances, and simultaneously moved forward, covering the whole territory as they went. It was agreed that if the children were found, guns should immediately be fired. In this manner they marched forward; every man's eye intently fixed upon every object his field of vision covered. They moved on with breathless anxiety till about nine o'clock, when the report of a gun sent a thrill of joy through every heart. Presently another and another gun gave assurance to hope, and brought the whole company around the rescued children.

It seems that a certain hunter, familiar at Mr. Mumford's, while eagerly searching for the lost ones, heard the little dog bark, that had strayed with and attended the children in their wanderings. He at once recognized the sound, and immediately bent his course towards it, and found the children sitting under some bushes. He gave the appointed signal, which brought together the whole company. With joy in every countenance, the multitude returned with them to their home. The mother clasped them in her arms and wept a flood of tears. It was a melting scene; strong, hardy men of the forest were overcome with emotion.

The children soon told their own story. They had wandered the first day in search of home, till night overtook them. Exhausted, they sat down, and the dark night gathered about them. The older one gathered a few leaves for a bed, and they laid down together, with little "Trip" (which was the dog's name), by the side of them. Presently "two big gray dogs," as they called them, "came and put their paws on a log," and looked over at them; but little "Trip," bristling up, ran and drove them off. These were undoubtedly wolves, that had followed their track. The next day they wandered about, gathering a few berries to satisfy their hunger. "My child, where did you sleep last night," inquired the mother of the youngest, who was not yet able to speak plainly. "Under a 'ittle geen tee" was the innocent reply. The elder sister said she cried in the night, because she was cold, and asked her to pull the clothes over her. They had become fearful of everything. They had heard frightful stories about the Indians, and were afraid of those who were searching for them, and would hide from them when they came near or heard their call. It is thought they never would have been found had it not been for the little dog that accompanied them.

VII. ROADS.

A few words are due in the history of this township with reference to the first roads here constructed. No State in the Union has manifested more enterprise in the construction of roads than Pennsylvania. As early as the year 1712 it was the custom of the proprietaries, and afterwards of the Commonwealth, to allow all purchasers of vacant lands an addition without charge, in the proportion of six acres for every one hundred purchased. This was given as a compensation for roads and highways that might afterwards be constructed by authority of the State. This custom has continued in all grants of vacant land since that time. The customary acre of Pennsylvania, therefore, in such grants, consisted of 169 perches and six-tenths of a perch; whereas the strict measure of this State makes the acre consist of 160 perches.

The first road through this township was intended to be a great highway for Western emigration. It was built by private enterprise, aided by State appropriation. The Act of Legislature for opening it was passed March 28, 1788. It was to be made sixty feet wide, beginning at Pocona Point, a place near Stroudsburg, and extend north to the State line. It was cut through in 1788-'89, but never thoroughly worked. The State appropriated £1,000 towards it. In this town it followed nearly the route of the present "Belmont and Easton Turnpike," and was called the "North and South Road." From Belmont it proceeded north until it intersected the State line. The "act" also provided for another road, to leave this "at or near Mount Ararat," and to be constructed westward to the mouth of the Tioga river. But as the Susquehanna river, with which the former was connected, furnished so good a substitute for this road, it was never constructed. This was a great and far-reaching project for that early day. It was de-

HISTORICAL DISCOURSE. 51

signed to open a great thoroughfare through the unsettled portions of the State, and, as the "act" says, "conduce to the immediate settlement of an extensive tract of country," and "by communication with other roads already begun, render Pennsylvania the most eligible route for emigrants from the Northern and Eastern parts of the United States." In 1791 the settlers in this town began opening a road to Great Bend. It left the North and South Road nearly opposite Mr. Stanton's house, and proceeded westward, varying from half a mile to a mile south of the present turnpike, which has taken its place. Soon after there was another road, which left the North and South Road from two to three miles south of Mr. Stanton's, and proceeding westward, intersected the road to Great Bend, in the western part of Herrick Township. From the fact that this road intersected the other two in the form of a brace, it was usually called the "Brace Road." It came down into the Lackawanna Valley, near Mr. Benjamin Smith's residence. Many of the settlers of Susquehanna County passed over this road. It was never worked much, and relinquished at an early day. There was another road early made and still in use, which left the North and South Road on the *east* side, about four miles south of this village, and came up by Mr. Silas Kellogg's improvement, passed Mr. Joseph Stearns', and continued north to Mr. John Tiffany's farm, now owned by Mr. Christopher. From this point a road was constructed *westward* to the brow of the hill near Mr. William Wright's residence, then passing southward down by Mr. Geer's log-house, near the large spring, and then over the Lackawaxen, a few rods above Mr. Baker's residence. As this was a prominent road previous to the construction of the turnpike which took its place, it may be of interest to notice the inhabitants on it, beginning with Mr. John Tiffany. On leaving his house westward was Nathan Rood, Solomon West, Henry Newton, Benjamin Newton, Silas Tanner; next, a frame schoolhouse; then Joseph Tanner and Benjamin Dix. As it passed Mr. Dix's, it bent southward, and passed down as before mentioned. Just before it reached the stream it connected with another road that came up in the direction of the present Bethany road, and passed the dwellings of Messrs. Benjamin King, Ruben Carr, and Elijah Dix. Here the two roads uniting, passed over the Lackawaxen. Then they parted to accommodate two taverns at the top of the hill, kept by Mr. Stanton and Mr. Mumford, on the north and south road.

There are five turnpikes, which either commence or pass through this township. The Cochecton and Great Bend Turnpike, incorporated March 29, 1804, passes through it from Cochecton to Great Bend.* The following terminate in this town: "Bethany and Dingman's Choice," incorporated March 2d, 1811.† "Belmont and Easton," incorporated March 13th, 1812. "Belmont and Ochquaga," incorporated February 26th, 1817. "Lackawaxen Turnpike," incorporated January 17th, 1828.

* See Appendix, No. 8. † See Appendix, No. 9.

VIII. ORIGIN AND PROGRESS OF THE TOWNSHIP.

At the time this place was settled, it was, together with this and the county of Pike, included in the undefined regions of the town of Upper Smithfield, in Northampton County. At that time, the elections for this region were held in the house of Nicholas Depuis, in the vicinity of Stroudsburg. The polls were so remote (about 70 miles) that no votes were ever cast by any of the people here at any election in that county. They were so isolated from all civil jurisdiction, that no tax was levied, and no officer reached them, or was appointed, with one exception: this was the appointment of Mr. Samuel Stanton, by the Governor, in 1796, to act as a Justice of the Peace here for Northampton County. Thus things continued till this town was organized, in 1798, the same year in which Wayne County was set off from Northampton. This county then embraced all of Pike County and nearly one half of Monroe. This was one of ten townships constituted by the Legislature with the county. The five following were in the present territory of Wayne County: Canaan, Palmyra, Buckingham, Damascus, Mount Pleasant. This township had originally a territory of twelve miles north and south, and eight miles east and west, containing about 96 square miles. It included one-seventh and five-tenths of the entire county. The territory first included in this county was divided into three election districts. The third and northern included all of the present Wayne County and about one half of Pike. This district comprised six of the original townships. In the same territory there are now nineteen townships and four boroughs. The polls for this district were opened in this town at the house of Elijah Dix, during the years 1798 and 1799. To this place all the inhabitants on the Waullenpaupack and north of the Shoholy Creek, came to vote. They came up the Lackawaxen to the junction of the Dyberry, where Honesdale now stands. This was then a dense, uninhabited wilderness. Leaving the stream, they proceeded through Bethany by marked trees, and so found their way to Mount Pleasant. Citizens on the Delaware found their way hither by bridle paths. Here, for the first time, the scattered inhabitants of the wilderness met from all parts of this extensive district to choose the State and county officers. The polls were held open in the log-house of Mr. Elijah Dix. It stood a few rods east of Mr. Ebenezer Richardson's late residence. This log-house served as a residence, a school-house, a meeting-house, and now for an election-house. It is to be regretted that not a single relic of this house is now to be found.* Previous to the organization of this town, the settlement was usually called Stantonville. In regard to the origin of the name it *now* bears, it is obvious that no created being gave it. The Hand that formed these hills and clothed them with their beauty, wrote its name. Man has only *read* it here. It could be called nothing else. The men who struck the first blow in the wilderness found it here. It is said that one

---

* A framed house now standing a few rods west of the old foundation, was built in 1801.

Robert L. Hooper, in surveying his lands here in 1775, while overlooking the township from one of the elevations of the Moosic Mountains, was charmed with its beauty, and exclaimed, "*This is Mount Pleasant.*" On this point there never has been a question. Mr. Stanton saw that the Creator had named it, and, therefore, the impropriety of connecting his own name with it. And what stranger even that overlooks these hills and valleys in their verdure, but must also say this town could be called by no other name?

About the time this village was becoming the centre of business for the township, a few individuals named it Centreville. It never was fully adopted, and has long since become obsolete.

By an act of Legislature of March 27, 1845, this village was incorporated as a borough, embracing a mile square, under the name of Pleasant Mount. On the 7th of May, 1855, that act was repealed, and the village was again merged into the township. The Post-Office, however, still retains the name of Pleasant Mount.

The slow progress made during the first period of this township did not meet the expectation of the early settlers. Some of them who had made large purchases on the expectation of a rapid growth, suffered embarrassment. This expectation, which had become general and confident, induced them to pay extravagant prices for land. At the date of the first settlement here this whole region had been surveyed, and was held by men who had bought to sell at an advanced price. They had projected and opened the North and South Road, which, it was expected, would become a great thoroughfare. Plans already entered upon would, it was thought, make two large places of business in this vicinity. One of these was on the Delaware, at Stockport, the other on the Susquehanna, at Harmony. These expectations, which were never realized, induced the first settlers to purchase at too high prices. Mr. Stanton paid for his first purchase at the rate of one hundred pounds per one hundred acres. He could have bought Government land at the same time at the rate of twenty pounds per one hundred acres.* The growth of the township has therefore, from its origin, been gradual, though uniform. Its population in 1800 was 188, which exceeded that of any other town then in this county It was not, however, as large, nor as favorably situated to secure a rapid settlement, as many others. It has been diminished on the northeast and south sides to form, or be added to, other townships. It now contains fifty-seven and a half square miles. The population of this town in 1850 was 1.737. At the present time it is about 2,000. The number of taxables in 1855 was 360.† The last assessment gives the following estimate of property:

Real Estate, . . .	$74,078 00
Personal Property, . .	24,056 00
Aggregate, ...	$98,134 00

* See "Act" of Oct. 3d, 1788, Sergeant's "Land Laws of Pennsylvania," page 274.

† When this town was organized in 1798, there were residing in it thirty-four taxables.

The greater part of the inhabitants are engaged in agriculture. Considerable attention is given to dairying. In 1850 there were made 35 tons of butter, and in 1855, 70 tons. Of grain there was raised in 1850,

   12,100 bushels of Oats.
   5,400 " Indian Corn.*
   6,831 " Buckwheat.

There are ten saw-mills in this town, which cut annually two million feet of lumber; three flouring and grist-mills, having nine run of stones, which grind annually 30,000 bushels of grain; three turning-mills, which use 225,000 feet of lumber; two wagon-shops, five blacksmith-shops, two tanneries, and one carding and cloth-dressing machine.

There are also five stores, in which there is an annual trade of $50,000.

IX. RELIGIOUS EVENTS.

As we have already seen, the Gospel was early preached in this town. The first minister of Christ who preached the Gospel here, was Elder David Jayne, who then lived on the Tunkhannock. He came by request of Samuel Stanton and others, in July, 1795. The next year, on the 28th of June, a Free Communion Baptist Church was organized. A number of persons of this denomination in New England had joined together, and agreed with Mr. Stanton to proceed into some new country and purchase a lot of land, and they would take portions of it and

* See Appendix, No. 10.

form a settlement. But on hearing of the isolated situation of his purchase, they all declined settling with him. Others, however, of this denomination, from New England, were induced to settle here, which led to the organization of this church. It was constituted with six members.* In the spring of 1793 the regular and public worship of God on the Sabbath was commenced, which has never ceased to the present day. Having no minister of the Gospel to preach to them, they read printed discourses. Among those often read, were the sermons of Whitfield and Stennett.

Missionaries, in passing through this region, would spend one or two Sabbaths and preach to the people of this new settlement. The Rev. Daniel Thatcher, a missionary of the General Assembly of the Presbyterian Church, visited them, and on the 9th of July, 1797, administered the Sacrament of the Lord's Supper. This was the first time this truly Christian ordinance was ever administered in this town.† It is spoken of in a record made of it by Mr. Stanton, as a very interesting and profitable season. Several other missionaries of the General Assembly, in passing through this region, tarried over Sabbath and preached to the people of this settlement. Among them we notice the names of Rev. Messrs. Aaron Condit, James Boyd, Asa Hillyer and Robert H. Chapman.

The first *resident* clergyman settled here in 1800. His name was Epaphras Thompson. He was from Bristol, Connecticut. He was a Close Commun-

* See Appendix, No. 11.   † See Appendix, No. 12.

ion Baptist. A few months after his arrival, he attempted to induce the Free Communion Church he found in this settlement to adopt the Close Communion faith. Failing, however, in this attempt, he united with them, and preached to them for several years. In 1806 Mr. Elijah Peck was ordained by this Church as a Gospel minister. In 1807 he, with Elder Thompson and seven or eight other members of this church, separated and formed a Close Communion Church, which became very numerous under his ministrations. Both of these churches declined, and were some years ago disbanded. No vestige of them now remains.

In 1806 the first Methodist clergyman preached in this township. This was the Rev. Annon Owen. He had a circuit extending from Wilksbarre through this region to the Delaware river. The first Methodist Society was organized the same year in the house of Abram Cramer. Among the various clergymen who have been successively appointed over this charge, we notice the Rev. George Peck, D. D., and the Rev. Benjamin Ellis.

On the 26th of January, 1814, a Congregational Church was organized in this town by the Rev. Ebenezer Kingsbury and Rev. Worthington Wright, missionaries of the Connecticut Missionary Society. It was organized with seventeen members in the house of the late John Tiffany. In 1831 this church changed its form of government, and became Presbyterian, which form it still retains. At first the church was supplied occasionally by missionaries. Public worship was, however, uniformly sustained when destitute of a minister. During the greater proportion of the early history of this church, they were able to support the public preaching of the Gospel by uniting with some neighboring church. The first pastor settled over this church was the Rev. Henry A. Boyce. He was installed July 8th, 1835. He labored but a little more than a year, when he was called away by death. Rev. Anthony McReynolds succeeded him as pastor, and remained about two years. The next pastor was the Rev. Daniel Higbie. After a very acceptable and useful pastorate of six years, he was called away by ill health, The *writer of this history* was the next succeeding pastor of this church. It is now upwards of ten years since he commenced his pastoral labors in this congregation.

A few years after the organization of this church, it became obvious that they must have a house of public worship. All the private houses where they had been accustomed to worship, had become " too strait" for them. A house was consequently built on the first North and South Road, east of the village, connecting the Newburg and Bethany turnpikes. Its size was 48 by 24 feet. It was formed by building an addition of twenty-four feet square to a school-house of the same size. The two parts were thrown into one by a swing partition. In this effort, all denominations cordially united. So perfectly did this plan commend itself to all the citizens, that the same week it was suggested all the materials were brought upon the ground, and during the next week it was so nearly completed, that it was occupied for the purpose intended on the following Sabbath. This was in the year 1822, and it was the first house of public worship ever built in this town. Poor as it might now be considered as a place of public worship, it was then regarded as a valuable accomplishment. Many persons from six to seven miles distant regularly worshipped in this house. It was common for many of them to walk this distance to and from the meeting. Some of them who still survive have their happiest seasons of religious worship associated with that old house.

> "How charming is the place
> Where my Redeemer, God,
> Unvails the glories of his face,
> And sheds his love abroad!"
>
> "There from his eyes I met the heavenly beam,
> That kindled in my soul this deathless flame."

The Presbyterian congregation erected a church edifice in 1830.* This building is 45 by 55 feet. With the exception of the church in Bethany,† this was the first Presbyterian Church built in Wayne County. It was refitted and improved in 1850 at a cost of $700. In 1833 a colony of 31 members went off from this church to form another church of the same denomination in an adjoining town.

In 1832 the Methodist Society erected a plain and commodious house of worship about two miles east of the village, on the Bethany turnpike, and dedicated it on the 4th of July of that year. It was refitted and greatly improved in 1851.

---

* A charter was granted them September 21st, 1831.

† The Presbyterian Church in Bethany was erected in 1823.

In 1835 there was a Roman Catholic Church erected in the northeast part of the town. Since its erection, their number has greatly increased. There is now a large congregation statedly meeting in that house.

A Sabbath School Society, auxiliary to the American Sunday School Union, was organized in 1833. This society became very efficient and useful in establishing schools in different parts of the town. It continued for many years to elicit an increasing interest. We are much indebted to its early efforts for the elevated position this cause has to the present time occupied in the hearts of this community.

There was also a Tract Society organized in the same year. Much was done by this society, while its purposes were carried out in circulating religious tracts among the families of the township.

A Bible Society, auxiliary to the Wayne County Bible Society, was organized in 1838. Vigorous efforts were made, by appointing visitors in every school district in town, to raise funds and circulate the Scriptures without note or comment. The first officers of the society were William R. Stone, President, and Anson Chittenden, sen., Vice-President.

There were early efforts made in this town in the cause of temperance. The first society, called the "Mount Pleasant Temperance Society," was organized on the 9th of February, 1830.* Mr. Jacob Eaton was the first president of the society, and Mr. William R. Stone, secretary. Mr. Stone continued to be an efficient and able secretary of this society for

* See Appendix, No. 13.

twenty years. It was organized on the principles of abstinence from distilled spirits; but in 1837 the pledge of total abstinence from all intoxicating drinks was adopted. When organized, the society had nine members :*

  In 1835 it had 240 members.
  " 1840 " 384 "
  " 1845 " 401 "
  " 1850 " 550 "

The whole number of names enrolled to the present time is 610.

X. COMMON SCHOOLS.

Though Pennsylvania has been tardy in waking to the importance of Common Schools, many of the towns in this part of the State have not overlooked their value. Without aid from the State they have erected school-houses, and supported schools, even while in the infancy of their existence. The first school in this town was taught by Miss Lucy Stearns in the summer of 1794. It was held in Mr. Elijah Dix's log-house. She had twelve scholars, and received six shillings a-week as her wages. The first male teacher that ever taught in this township was Mr. John Tyler. He taught in the winter of 1799 and 1800. His school was in a log building which had been erected and occupied by Mr. Geer, but which then having no family in it, was used for the school. This was the only school in town, and num-

* See Appendix, No. 13.

bered about twenty-five scholars. The next winter a school was taught by Mr. Richard Perkins, on the old road running north of the village.

The *first framed* school-house was built in 1804.* It was the next building eastward of Joseph Tanner's residence. The first school in it was taught by Mr. Truman Wheeler.

In 1834 the State passed a law for a general system of education by Common Schools. In the same year there was a Board of School Directors chosen in this town under that law. The first officers were Truman Wheeler, President, and William R. Stone, Secretary. There are now in this town fourteen Common Schools, and 500 scholars. The school-houses are generally well built and commodious. One is of stone, one of brick, and others of wood, well finished and painted.

There have never been permanent provisions made in this town for a higher education than what is obtained in the Common Schools. We notice several, however, who were born and spent their youth here, that have overcome obstacles, and with an education more or less extensive, have entered some of the professions. These are Rev. Wesley Miller, a clergyman in the Methodist Episcopal Church. He graduated at the Wesleyan University in 1848. We may also notice Mr. Jacob Eaton, who is a member of the Presbyterian Church in this place, and also of the Theological Department of Yale College. He is now

---

* The author has been informed that a log school-house was erected in 1798. It stood in the vicinity of Philo Spencer's residence.

about entering the last year of his preparatory studies for the ministry. In the legal profession, we notice Mr. Henry L. Palmer, who is practicing law in Milwaukie, Wisconsin. Of physicians, we notice Drs. Lowell Lillibridge, who died in California, Solomon Essary, who is practicing medicine near Chester, New York, Charles T. Wheeler, who is a practicing physician in Indiana, William H. Wheeler, who is now dead, and Jirah Rogers, who is practicing medicine in Wisconsin.

For a greater diffusion of knowledge among the people, there has been for many years a circulating library in town. It consists at the present time of 157 volumes.

XI. RESIDENT PHYSICIANS.

The first resident physician in this township was Dr. Asa Parks. He lived in a house which stood east of Mr. John F. Sherwood's residence, on the farm now owned by Mr. Arthur. The old chimney stack is still to be seen. He resided here three or four years, and was considered a good physician. He was afterwards a successful practitioner in Montrose for many years. Before he came here the people employed Dr. Chandler, who resided in Gibson, about sixteen miles west of this place. His ride extended beyond here twenty miles to the Delaware river.

The next resident physician was Dr. John P. Kennedy. He came in 1811, and left in 1815. He lived in a house which stood nearly opposite Mr. John F. Sherwood's.

In 1814 Drs. Jonathan French and Uriel Wright began their residence in this town. Dr. French was from Newburyport in Massachusetts, where he had very successfully devoted his efforts to his profession for fifteen years. He was a skilful physician, possessing a finished education, and refined in his deportment. He came here to relieve himself from an exhausting practice. He designed, also, to engage in the lumber business. He had, however, while here, many professional calls. Not succeeding in lumbering to his expectation, he remained but two or three years. Dr. Wright, who came at the same time, was then a young man from Berkshire County, Massachusetts. He has consequently practiced medicine here forty-one years. Part of this time he has had a ride of fifteen or twenty miles around, often through a desolate wilderness. Though the frosts of many winters have whitened his few remaining hairs, he may still be seen breasting the storm with a resolute spirit to reach the sick and suffering.

In 1834 Dr. Edwin Eldridge came, and had a limited practice of about two years.

In 1837 Dr. Rodney Harmes began his practice of medicine in this place. He was from Sullivan County, New York, and had recently entered upon his profession. He still resides here as one of the physicians of this township.

Dr. Frederick Tracy began the practice of medicine here in 1851. After a practice of about two years he removed his residence from this place.

XII. HUNTERS.

There is another class of men who deserve a notice in the history of this town. They do so from the fact that their work is now done. If, therefore, it is not written, it must be left to an uncertain tradition. I refer to the *hunter*. There are emergencies in a hunter's life which educe the qualities of the man. There are few men who are or can be hunters. A thoughtless boy can shoot an innocent robin or a merry squirrel, who gives you a lively chirp before he dodges into his underground room : but he is *no hunter*. There are emergencies in a hunter's life which require the most sterling traits of character, such as would make him a Leonidas or a Bonaparte, if in their circumstances. He must be a man of the utmost coolness in the midst of the most terrific scenes, quick and judicious in his movements, and of indomitable perseverance and bravery. The men who have proved these qualities in conflict with the fierce animals of the wilderness deserve our notice.

The first instance, though somewhat amusing, shows the tenacity with which a hunter will cling to his prey. It seems Mr. John Tiffany and Mr. Elijah Peck were hunting deer, and shot at a large buck. He fell to the ground. Mr. Tiffany immediately ran to cut his throat and remove the blood. When he had grasped his horns, with one foot on each side of his body, the animal instantly rose with him upon his back, and ran off at the top of his speed. He still clung to him, and vanished in the distance, crying out to his companion, "'Lijah! 'Lijah!! 'Lijah!!! But in that perilous flight Elijah could afford him no assistance. He soon relinquished his grasp, and was very unceremoniously alighted. He was found by his companion uninjured.

Mr. George McMullen settled in this town in 1800, and is of Scotch descent. He is tall, bony, yet compactly built, has a Roman nose, broad capacious mouth, a dark expressive eye, which is usually restless in its socket. He is animated in conversation, commanding in his general appearance, and disdains to be outdone. He has the natural qualities for a successful hunter. He has engaged in it more or less the greater part of his life. He has not done it for the profit of it so much as because he is passionately fond of it. Though now in his seventieth year, he will travel from ten to fifteen miles a day in pursuit of a deer. He is full of animation in this his favorite sport. Said he a few days ago, after returning from a chase, "The *smell* of the woods excites me when I have my rifle in my hand. I am ready for anything." His life is full of stirring incidents. He has had many bloody battles with the ferocious animals of this county in its wild state. He will entertain you for hours in relating them with such vivacity and excitement that you will think yourself in the midst of them. A few of these must serve the present occasion. On one of his hunting excursions he was out with another hunter and two dogs. They discovered a panther, and the dogs treed him. When they came up, he saw him with his enormous body stretched from limb to limb. His fierce eyes glared wildly down upon his foes. But our hunter with great deliberation levelled his rifle. Instantly the panther jumped upon a large hemlock limb, which being a little rotten, broke, and he fell in a place surrounded with fallen trees. Here the dogs closed in for a battle. At the first blow the panther struck one of the dogs, and tore the entire flesh from one side of his jaw, which sent him howling through the woods. The other, of "better pluck," grabbed the panther by the neck for a death-struggle. Our hunter saw his favorite dog dreadfully torn. Blood flowed from both combatants in a fearful manner. He called for his comrade's ax with which to end the fierce battle. But, alas! his companion stood with ghastly countenance, terror-stricken, and seemed not to know what he said. He, therefore, went to him, and seized his *loaded rifle*, and rushed to the scene of conflict. Watching his opportunity amid their writhing struggles, he put the muzzle of the rifle at the heart of the panther so as not to injure his dog, and thus ended the battle. After the death of the panther, so deeply and firmly were his claws imbedded in the neck of the dog, he was obliged to cut the cords of his paw to extract them.

But this is not the only conflict he has had with this kind of animal. On another occasion he was out alone in one of his favorite hunts. His attention was caught by a heavy rustling and crackling of limbs, mingled with a deep growl. He hastened to the place, and found an enormous panther fighting with a bear. Unobserved, he watched their attacks. He saw the panther rush upon the bear, grab her by the neck, when she would fall and hold the panther by the fore-paws, and tear him with her hind-feet, so that the skin and blood flew out at every stroke. He would soon let go his hold, yet exasperated to the highest degree, he would clinch the bear again. At the third onset our hunter thought *he* would have a share in the fight. He very deliberately discharged his rifle at the panther, when instantly he left the bear and came bounding at him, enraged to frenzy. He declares that the eyes of the panther were like balls of fire, and his teeth of the bigness of his thumb. As the maddened animal was about to spring upon him, he, eying him sharply, swung his rifle, and gave one of his terrific yet characteristic howls which brought the panther to a stand about a rod from him. He continued to swing his rifle, and eye him fiercely, with *such* a growl as George McMullen *only* can make. The panther made round him ready to spring, yet cowered by fear, until the bear, who had been defending her whelps from the panther, came and *again* fell upon him. At this instant he attempted to re-load, but in his hurry he unconsciously put the ball in *first*. He declares it is the only time he ever lost self-possession in all his conflicts and adventures with wild beasts. But the bear having worsted the panther and drove him off, came back fiercely upon *him*. He snapped his rifle, but to his astonishment it missed fire. There was no alternative but a close fight. He began to swing his rifle as the bear approached, and raise one of his inimitable howls. He had always a knife ready for such emergencies; but before called to use it, the bear heard her whelps, which the panther had treed, coming down and made off for them. But he would not give it up so. He was determined to carry home the bear with her whelps. He repeatedly primed his rifle, but to his utter astonishment it missed fire. There was no other way but to go home in disappointment. Not until he had taken his rifle to pieces did he discover his unconscious mistake.

At another time his spirit was roused by some wolves which had made depredations upon the flocks in this town. He tracked them over the Lackawanna into Susquehanna County, and found their den far away from any human habitations. Not being able to draw them out, he prepared to have a battle with them in their own den. So, setting down his rifle at the mouth of the den, and grasping his knife, he, down upon his hands and knees, made his way in through the narrow passes of projecting rocks. He found on his arrival that, contrary to his expectation, the old wolves were not at home. But perceiving in that dark abode a nest of half-grown cubs, he grabbed one, drew him out, and killed him. Encouraged by his success, he went in again, grabbed another, who, not so willing to be dragged out in this manner, bit his wrist badly; but finding that this did not relieve him from the death grasp around his heels, he made a most pitiable and deafening outcry which roused the old wolves. No sooner had he reached the mouth of the den with the crying cub and ended his troubles, than they were seen coming with all possible vengeance. He immediately grasped his rifle and took his stand. Not being able to make his rifle bear upon them as they came up, they snapped at him and passed by. Again they wheeled and came at him, but he defended their attack. They then parted, one to attack him on one side and the other on the other side. As the enraged mother came snarling with her bare teeth, he deliberately discharged a ball into her jaws. Then instantly turning upon the other and yelling in defiance at him, he was so intimidated as to make good his retreat. He then plunged into the den again and brought out every cub, and when he had counted the dead he found nine cubs and their mother, regretting most of all that *one* should have escaped. What becomes of the lauded adventure of General Putnam into the wolf's den when compared with that of George McMullen? But we must not *dwell longer* upon these fearless encounters. His life is full of them. He has often traversed this county in this his favorite sport. At one time he was in the wilderness in the north part of it thirteen successive nights, without seeing a human person during the time. It was his custom, when young, to teach school during the winter. Before going to his school he would have a hunt. One autumn he killed sixty-five deer, eleven bears, six red foxes, and nine martens. He then went down to the Susquehanna river, near the Wyoming valley, and taught school during the winter.

Mr. John Wrighter settled in this town in 1812. He is of German descent. His father was a native of Bavaria. He has a tall, heavy-built frame. His features are all well developed. His movements are slow, but firm and forcible. His mind, partaking of his bodily characteristics, is well balanced—acts with great deliberation and perseverance, and is not moved by difficulties or dangers. He has cultivated a farm, and devoted but a part of his time to hunting. His success is owing more to his calm and fearless manner of meeting wild animals, than from any dexterity.

On one occasion, while hunting, he saw the head of a large buck peering up from behind an obstacle. He shot, and the deer fell. Dropping his gun, he ran up to make sure of him; but, when within a step or two, the wounded buck rose upon his enemy. An enraged buck is a most dangerous animal to meet. His remarkable strength and agility *combined*, make him a formidable foe. Throwing forward his horns, with every bristle erect, he made a pass at him. But, with great coolness, he evaded his blow, and grabbed his horn. Then came " the tug of war." For some time they fought in close combat. The buck, brandishing his antlers, would have been glad to have plunged them into his foe and tossed him into the air. But he found the iron sinews of the old German too strong for him. His cool, deliberate mode of warfare was more than a match for the sprightly buck. His strength was soon exhausted, and our hunter, who had long aimed to throw his combatant with his *feet from him*—for he had no thought of being raked with his sharp hoofs—now succeeded. He laid him across a log, which gave him an opportunity to draw his knife and end the conflict.

On another occasion he tracked a bear and some whelps far into the wilderness. While in pursuit he came suddenly upon the old bear at the mouth of her den. He had no sooner lodged his rifle ball in her body than she wheeled, and the dog made after her. But the commotion *without* alarmed the cubs *within*. They came rushing to the mouth of the den, when they were met by the old German, who grabbed one by the neck. He thought he could hug as hard as a young bear. But he soon found that he had "caught a Tartar." The little fellow proved to be as long-winded as his antagonist. But the stalwart hunter had been accustomed to these close fights. He had no thought of making compromises with young Bruin. A few more struggles brought this " fast youth" up against a log, where our hunter, releasing one hand, drew his knife and ended the battle. The young cub weighed fifty pounds.

It would seem that *such* a victory would have satisfied German ambition for *that day*. But, on his way home, he fell upon another track, which soon brought him to a cave or den among the rocks. He entered the mouth of it, and saw, about twenty feet before him, the glaring eye-balls of old Bruin, who had retired to her dark lair. Aiming at the space between the glaring eye-balls, hoping there might be brains there, he sent his leaden bullet on its message of death. After the smoke had passed away he crawled in, knife in hand, to reconnoitre the field and bring off the trophies of victory, if there should be any. As he advanced, he discovered that the enemy were not all dead, and that it might be safer for him to retreat to a place where he could have a fairer field. Accordingly, having returned, he took his rifle, and, re-entering, he again saw two eye-balls in that dark retreat rolling wildly at him. Seeing nothing very agreeable in their motion, he soon treated them to the same material he had before done. The smoke having removed, he re-entered, to count and recover the dead. Creeping cautiously, with knife in hand, he discovered now no fiery eye-balls—no movement—no signs of life. He at length laid his hand *firmly* on his prey; but life was extinct. He dragged out an old bear with her cub.

XIII. MRS. SARAH BENJAMIN.

There is a woman in this town who, on account of her extreme age, claims a notice in this discourse. Her name is Sarah Benjamin. Her maiden name was Sarah Mathews. She was born in Goshen, Orange County, New York, on the 17th of November, 1745. She was, therefore, 110 years old on Saturday last. She has had three husbands. The first was Mr. William Read. He served in the Revolutionary war, and was in the army in the early part of the struggle. He died of a wound received while in Virginia. Her second husband was Mr. Aaron Osborne, of Goshen, Orange County, New York. He *also* was in the army of the Revolution, and survived the war. She was with him during a part of the time he was in the army, as will presently appear. She has had five children. Her youngest is now *sixty-seven* years old. She settled in this town with her last husband, Mr. John Benjamin, about the year 1822. He died in the year 1826. She has now in this place her great-great-grandchild, which has descended from her youngest daughter. Including herself, this child belongs to the fifth generation. These generations, still unbroken by death, have often *met* in this town. But what is still more remarkable is, that none of them have the vivacity which she, even now, has in conversation. Few persons in the *prime* of *life*, can throw so much animation into a brief interview, as this relic of a past age. She has naturally great energy of mind and body. She is bold, fearless, very cheerful, and ready for a joke with any one. She has enjoyed remarkably good health all her life. She says she was never sick but once. She then sent for the physician of this place, who left her some medicine. But, after he was gone, she, not liking the smell of it, says she "threw the dirty stuff into the fire, and *then had to pay for it.*" The doctor never loses a good joke from her, on account of it, to the present day.

Her parents moved into this State when she was quite young. They resided at Minisink. She has a distinct recollection of crossing the Delaware, and of being lifted up in the arms of one of the men as they approached the shore, to pick some beautiful clusters of ripe strawberries.

From her youth, until over forty years of age, she was in the midst of the rough and stirring scenes of the border warfare and Revolutionary struggle. Her temperament was such, that she could be no idle spectator. She entered very deeply into those trying events. She distinctly recollects the family of Mr. Broadhead, whose sons, in 1755, boldly resisted a party of 200 Indians, making their house a fort. She has often been in this house, and says it was built of stone. She was acquainted with Nicholas Depuis and his family, and will now repeat a piece of poetry, of about twenty lines, written concerning an unhappy, though somewhat romantic marriage of his son. She was in the vicinity of Minisink when Brant, the Indian chief, led a party of Indians and Tories through that settlement, scalping the inhabitants and burning their houses. She entered very deeply into the spirit of the Revolutionary war. She was confident of its success, and had no fears of danger. After her second marriage, in the latter part of the war, she accompanied her husband in the army. During their marches, she made herself useful in preparing food, and when not thus employed, engaged in sewing for the officers and men. She was, however, **ready for *any* service** which circumstances seemed to require. When the army were engaged in embarking some heavy ordnance at Kingsbridge on the Hudson, ostensibly to attack New York, then in the hands of the enemy, it was necessary to do it in the night, and to place sentries around, lest they should be observed, or taken by surprise. Her husband having been placed as a sentinel, she came and took his place, with overcoat and gun, that he might help load the heavy artillery. Soon, however, General Washington came round to examine the outposts, and seeing something in her appearance a little unusual, said : " Who placed you *here?*" She promptly replied, in her characteristic way, "Them that had a *right* to, Sir!" He, apparently pleased with her independent and patriotic spirit, passed on.

She accompanied the army with her husband to the South, and was present at the siege of Yorktown and surrender of Cornwallis. During the battle, she was busy in carrying water to the thirsty and relieving the wants of the suffering. When passing where the bullets of the enemy were flying, she met General Washington, who said : " Young woman, are you not afraid of the bullets?" She promptly and pleasantly replied : " The bullets will never cheat the gallows." She says the General smiled, and passed on.

Such is her extraordinary energy—even in her extreme age—that she will now relate the events of those days with all the vivacity of youth. Though she receives a pension from Government for her support, she can never sit down without having some *work* in her hands. She tenaciously holds to the old practice of carding and spinning wool. She says she " is no friend to machines that save labor and *make people lazy.*" At this extreme age, she takes the wool in the fleece, cards, spins, doubles, often with three threads, and knits it. The fineness and beauty of the yarn is a wonder and admiration to all. Not a young lady can be found able to compete with her in the beauty and value of her work. Until quite recently, she has had all the ambition of youth to spin every day her "*day's work*." Not long since, in calling upon her, we found her spinning wool at a "little wheel." he is not now able to spin at the "large wheel." Without stopping her wheel, she says, pleasantly : "I must finish my day's work." We sat down by her side, to witness with astonishment, in the motions of that aged form, what we never expect to see in another. Having finished the roll in her hand, she arose as usual, and welcomed us. That wheel she has used sixty years, and, after having been somewhat repaired, now turns out under her hand good work Her work has also been exhibited in the American Institute, and received very flattering notices. Her yarn and stockings are in great demand. Persons from a distance, visiting this town, do not fail to call on her for a specimen of her yarn or stockings. She sent a beautiful specimen of fine woollen stockings to the World's Fair in New York. The wool for them was taken in the fleece, and the entire work was done by herself. We also notice that, at our county fair, last month, she took the premium on linen cloth.

She still keeps up the practice of making yearly visits to her old friends in town. These visits are usually made on foot. If at a distance, she is willing to ride, but disdains the effeminate etiquette of being *helped* into a carriage. Your speaker was permitted to welcome her to the parsonage, at a donation visit, one year ago last January. It will not be a breach of propriety here, to say that he received from her a beautiful pair of stockings, made from the fleece with her own hands. The yarn, though fine, is composed of three threads. He has never seen the occasion which could justify him in treading upon the memento of such an *aged* friend, without committing a sacrilegious act. At this visit, two other aged females were present : one seventy-three, and the other sixty-nine. All seemed to enjoy the interview. But the oldest seemed to be the youngest, and the youngest the oldest.

Ten days from that visit the youngest died. At the close of this interview, being about to have a season of worship, our aged friend, then one hundred and eight years old, sang, with a clear, distinct voice, the following verse :

> "The day is past and gone,
> The evening shades appear—
> Oh, may we all remember well
> The night of death draws near."

And then knelt with us during prayer.

But, most of all, am I happy to say here, she appears to have the consolations and hopes of the Saviour's love. She has often said : " This is all my comfort." She is ready and waiting to depart. The infirmities of age seem to be growing upon her. May the kind and gracious Saviour bear her aged form gently downwards to the tomb, and gather her redeemed spirit into the bosom of his love.

I have now finished my plan for writing the history of this township. I have carried you through the lights and shades of life as here developed. This may be very imperfectly done. But I am reminded that there is another history, written by an *unerring hand*. It is a history of thought, of conduct, and of character. The leaves of that history are on high. Our fathers have many of them gone to meet it. A few of them yet stand waiting at the river of death.

Soon, fellow-citizens, shall we *all* appear where a different history of life will be read from that which I have written. *There*, mere earthly names and distinctions are nothing. Character and the awards of that life are tried by a different standard from that found in human records. When we meet in *that* world, and *those* books shall be opened, may we all find our names written in the Lamb's book of life.

APPENDIX.

NO. I.

MILITARY EVENTS.

UNTIL after the war of 1812, military honors were sought for and highly prized. To be a *captain* even was an enviable distinction. There was no military organization north of the Shoholy Creek until after Wayne County was constituted. This organization took place at Willsonville, in 1798. Mr. Samuel Stanton was, at this time and place, elected Major of the battalion. He held this office two years, when he resigned, and Mr. Joseph Tanner succeeded him. Mr. Tanner was succeeded by Mr. Jason Torrey. This office was held during the latter part of the war of 1812 by Mr. Luther Starks.

The following persons held the office of Captain until after this war, and in the following .order: John Tiffany—Elijah Peck—Thomas Mumford—Chandler Tiffany—Luther Starks, and Harry Mumford. The first battalion-training in this town was in 1813. The first regimental training was in 1804, under Colonel Asa Stanton. There was also another here, under Colonel Harry Mumford, who received his commission in 1828. There have been various military elections here for battalion and regimental officers. The battalion covered this county, and the regiment covered this and Susquehanna Counties.

NO. II.

GRAVE-YARDS.

There are three public grave-yards in this town. All of them are well protected by substantial stone walls, and are held as town property. These are located in the southern, central, and northern parts of the township. The land for the central yard was given, one-half by Mr. Benjamin King, and the other half was designed as a donation to the town by Mr. Silas Kellogg, but, by an oversight, he did not reserve it in the sale of the adjoining land, and the town received it as a gift from the purchaser, Mr. Benjamin Wheeler.

The first burial in this ground took place in June, 1802. The individual was a daughter of Mr. Abram Cramer, who had recently been married to Mr. Joseph Reeder. She was well known and highly esteemed by all. The funeral was held in a grove on the east side of the grave-yard. A large number of people were present, who listened to a discourse by the Rev. Epaphras Thompson, from Revelation xiv. 13: "Blessed are the dead which die in the Lord," &c.

The grave-yard situated in the south part of the

town, was first occupied for this purpose in 1826. The individual first buried was Mr. Gilbert Horton. The land was given by Mr. David Horton, and consists of about one-half of an acre.

The third public grave-yard is in the north part of the town. The land was given by Mr. Samuel Brooking, and consists of about one acre. The first burial was on Nov. 14, 1850. Several graves, located on private property, were opened, and the bodies interred in the yard. Prayer was offered on the occasion, and an address, appropriate to the opening of this ground, was delivered by the Rev. Samuel Whaley.

NO. III.

MORTALITY.

The following notice of the deaths in this town for the thirteen years past, may be of some service, as well as interest, in the history of this town. The author is indebted for it to Mr. William R. Stone:

In 1843 there were . . . 20 deaths.
" 1844, " . . . 19 "
" 1845, " . . . 14 "
" 1846, " . . . 6 "
" 1847, " . . . 9 "
" 1848, " . . . 46 "
" 1849, " . . . 19 "
" 1850, " . . . 11 "
" 1851, " . . . 8 "

APPENDIX.

In 1852 there were	. . .	13 deaths.
" 1853, "	. . .	20 "
" 1854, "	, . .	20 "
" 1855, "	. . .	10 "

It will be seen from this table that the year 1848 was remarkable for its number of deaths. The cause of this will be seen by giving an extract from the annual discourse of the pastor of the Presbyterian Church in this town, delivered Jan. 7, 1849:

"During the last year there were forty-six deaths in this town. This is a very unusual number. For the five years preceding this last, the average number of deaths in this town was thirteen and six-tenths for each year. This certainly is a small number for the population. Placing the population at 1700, and the deaths in this town, for the five years past, have been one for every one hundred and twenty-five persons. This surely is a small number. There are few places that can be said to be as healthful."

The deaths in this State, according to the census of 1850, are in the proportion of one to every eighty-one of the population. "The ratio of deaths in the city of New York, which is called a healthful city, is one to every 36 or 37 of its population. Whereas, in this town, for five years past we have had only one death to every one hundred and twenty-five of the population. Last year, however, which proved to be a very sickly season, there has been one death to every thirty-seven of our population. This large increase of deaths in this town was caused by the epidemic which prevailed here during the months of August and September. This will be seen from the number of deaths in each month. In January, one ; in February, two ; in March, one ; in April, two ; in May, one ; in June, one ; in July, three ; in August, seventeen ; in September, twelve ; in October, two ; in November, three, and in December, one. Thus it will be seen that the epidemic was mostly confined to August and September. With the exception of these months, we have but seventeen deaths in town during the year. This epidemic—the dysentery—has never before been known to prevail in this town. The same thing may be seen from the various causes which have produced it, and their relative number. They are as follows : Four infants, whose disease was unknown ; croup, two ; pleurisy, one ; parturition, one ; inflammation of bowels, one ; chronic rheumatism, two ; consumption, one ; fever, two ; worms, one ; lung-fever, one ; old age, one ; asthma, one ; cholera-morbus, two ; dysentery, twenty-six. Thus it will be seen that the greatest number of deaths has been caused by this disease, and that, aside from this, no one disease has prevailed—two being the highest number from any other disease. It will also be seen, from the following statement, that this disease has proved most fatal among children. Died, during the past year, at the age of five, and younger, nineteen ; between five and twenty, seven ; between twenty and forty, nine ; between forty and sixty, four ; and from sixty and older, seven. There have been nearly as many deaths among children of five years old and

APPENDIX. 87

younger, as those of all other ages. With these facts before us, it is extremely difficult to form any conclusion as to the *cause* of this unusual mortality. Many things have been conjectured, but it is evident that no one cause can account for it. A variety of circumstances expose the system to disease. The same epidemic prevailed during the last season in many parts of our country, and in its healthiest localities. But, whatever may have been the immediate cause, we know there is one First Great Cause, who rules all intermediate causes. Sickness and death are at His disposal. In His hands are all the springs of life."

NO. IV.

This township is elevated from sixteen to seventeen hundred feet above tide-water. The following table, prepared with much care, for the different months of the years 1846 and 1849, will show the character of the seasons, temperature and variations:

THERMOMETRICAL OBSERVATIONS AT MOUNT PLEASANT VILLAGE.

	Months.	At Sunrise.			At 2 P. M.			Greatest Variations.		Least Variations.		Mean Variation.
		Max.	Min.	Mean.	Max.	Min.	Mean.					
1846.	July	68	48	55.8	96	56	77.9	20th	from 60 to 90	15th	from 50 to 58	17.7
	Aug.	68	52	60.3	92	66	87.8	3d	" 64 " 92	15th	" 63 " 73	20.5
	Sept.	72	40	49.4	94	42	69.2	17th	" 46 " 70	28th	" 40 " 42	15.5
	Oct.	58	18	40.0	76	29	54	12th	" 28 " 58	31st	" 32 " 36	14
	Nov.	54	10	33.9	68	15	40	18th	" 32 " 53	25th	" 27 " 28	7.1
	Dec.	41	7	20	38	12	25.6	24th	" 7 " 25	9th	" 26 " 24	7.2
1849.	Jan.	42	−10	13.2	40	−6	20	12th	" −8 " 24	2d	" 1 " 2	7.7
	Feb.	27	−10	12.5	46	5	22.8	28th	" 20 " 46	5th	" 25 " 22	12.3
	Mar.	42	11	23.4	54	25	35.2	4th	" 11 " 38	14th	" 26 " 28	13.2
	April	50	11	28.1	63	23	41.9	30th	" 29 " 61	8th	" 32 " 32	15.2
	May	60	28	42.6	73	34	55.3	4th	" 46 " 73	25th	" 44 " 46	13.4
	June	70	38	57.6	87	48	71.5	27th	" 57 " 85	16th	" 66 " 67	14.2
	July	70	43	60.3	90	60	78	29th	" 53 " 85	14th	" 70 " 72	18.4

In 1847, Thermometer stood the lowest, Jan. 22d −3.
" 1848, " " " " 11th −15.
" 1854, " " " Dec. 19th −5.
" 1855, " " " Feb. 6th −24.

NO. V.

The Dyberry is called in the oldest surveys of this region, the "northeast branch of the Lackawaxen." From various accounts, it is probable it received its present name as follows:

At an early period, a Mr. Dye began improvements on this stream, a little above the present village of Honesdale. He felled some of the timber and girdled some. In this state he left it, and did not return. In a few years it was covered with bushes, which bore a bountiful supply of luxuriant berries. This was called Dye's berry-field—or Dye's berries. Hence, Dyberry. This name was given to the stream, upon whose margin the field was located.

NO. VI.

The following is a copy of some verses written by Mr. Samuel Stanton. As they have a historical interest, and embody the opinion then generally entertained, that there would be a great western thoroughfare through this region, they are here inserted. The author is indebted for them to Hon. Paul S. Preston, who has also kindly furnished other documents of interest and value.

The most that was then expected was a good turnpike road. Little did they think of a great iron railway connecting New York City and Lake Erie. Had the writer seen the majestic arch of the Erie Railroad, which now spans the Cascade gulf, and the ponderous trains, laden with a nation's wealth, forced on their way by the iron horse, his poetic genius would have kindled with new fire.

"A few Lines of Poetry, attempted on seeing and assisting in building the town of Harmony, on the Susquehanna River, Aug. 2, 1789.

I.

" When I see towns and cities rise,
It fills my mind with sweet surprise
To find what man may do:
To see bright genius displayed,
And deserts turned to marts for trade,
Is sure a pleasant show.

II.

" In contemplation rapt, methinks
I see on Susquehanna's banks,
Where savages long rov'd,
A pretty town in order stand,
Stored with the riches of the land,
Possess'd by men belov'd.

III.

" Sweet, happy place, called Harmony.
Strangers must say, when they pass by,
The Founder they approve ;
Who from a forest wild did raise
A seat where men may spend their days
In friendship, peace, and love.

IV.

"Here nature, industry, and art,
Join—and their various powers exert
In several different ways.
The builders do cut down and hew
The pines which unregarded grew,
And famous houses raise.

V.

"Each tradesman here may have employ,
 And the oppressed are filled with joy,
  That virtue has a home.
 The vicious here no count'nance find,
 But the distressed are used kind,
  And here the honest come.

VI.

"Here health and peace do walk the round—
 Plenty springs from the well-till'd ground,
  Where honest farmers live :
 More happy far than warriors are,
 The fruits of their industry share,
  And to the needy give.

VII.

"From the high rock with lofty roar,
 The Cascade stream did useless pour,
  But now its use we know.
 Millers and clothiers it maintains—
 The smith and potash-maker gains
  A living by its flow.

VIII.

"The gardens it from drought defends,
 And what none use still downward tends,
  To join the flood below.
 There boats do find a pleasant road,
 And their rich treasures they unload,
  And safely come and go.

IX.

"How curiously the streets are plann'd,
 How thick the stores and houses stand—
  How full of goods they are!
 From north and south the merchants meet,
 Have what they wish for most complete,
  And to their homes repair.

X.

"Drinker is worthy of esteem,
Who plann'd and brought about the scheme
  That I this day do see.
May blessings all thy plans attend—
While thou art still the poor man's friend,
  Thou art beloved by me.

XI.

"And Preston, too, who takes the care,
May he in all the blessings share,
  And always have a friend;
And have a long and prosperous life,
A worthy woman for a wife,
  To love and to defend.

XII.

"The workmen who assist to raise
The town, must have a little praise,
  And some good wish bestow'd;
May they live long—be good and great—
Be bless'd in person and estate,
  And walk the right-hand road."

NO. VII.

The following letter was received too late to be used in the Discourse, but which contains some statements worthy of notice. It was written by a native of this town, who spent his youth in this place:

GIBSON, *Jan.* 29*th*, 1856.

REV. MR. WHALEY:

DEAR SIR: I have delayed replying to your note, hoping to be able to give the desired information; but, up to this time, have not been able to do so. * * * By the way, short as my life has been, I have some recollections of the men of those early times—of Samuel Stanton in particular. Well do I remember accompanying my parents to religious meetings in the barn of Samuel Stanton, somewhere on Belmont Hill. No easy-cushioned seats in those days. We boys were disposed of in the manger, or on the scaffold. Well do I remember that the good matrons of those days—yea, and the young women (no ladies then)—would carefully carry their shoes, when going to meeting, till near the house, before they would put them on. The more favored few, who first came out with wagons of a most *uncomfortable* build—a plain board box upon a stiff, unyielding axle—were then considered aristocratic. In short, the real and pressing wants of the times left no room for indulgence in luxuries. When we go back in imagination, and try to contemplate what our first settlers endured, the thought is interesting and melancholy. For long, long years, they labored on in their wilderness-homes—the deep snows of the dreary winter shutting them out from all communication with the more favored world. Some pressing want compels the father to leave his little family for a season—his stay may be necessarily protracted—sickness visits his little family. For long, long days and weary nights, his companion watches over the sick ones, and with painful anxiety awaits his return. No friendly voice salutes her ear—no physician is at her command. But the actors of those trying times are gone—their history is buried with them. It is well that the little which can be gathered up should be preserved.

A knowledge of what our fathers endured may be useful to us, and to those who live after we are gone. I think the undertaking very commendable, and wish you much success in its prosecution.

Respectfully, Yours, &c.,

N. E. KENNEDY.

NO. VIII.

The following facts concerning this road are taken from a report made by the company to the Senate, in 1822. They may be of interest, to show the magnitude and value of this road in the first period of its existence—as well as the enterprise of the inhabitants:

"The length of this road is fifty miles. Beginning at the Delaware river, it passes through the towns of Damascus, Lebanon, and Mount Pleasant, in Wayne County, and Gibson, New Milford, and Great Bend, in Susquehanna County. It was begun in 1806, and finished in 1811. The act of incorporation provided for 1,000 shares of $50 each, with power to increase the number of shares, so as to fulfil the intention of the act. The number of shares taken was 1,657. The capital stock, therefore, amounted to $82,850. The road received no assistance from the State. It was built by individual enterprise—most of the stock was taken on the line of the road. It was constructed twenty feet wide. The materials are, earth, stone, lime, and timber. Its form was convex, being about four inches higher in the centre than at the sides

APPENDIX. 95

During the three first years, it paid a debt of $11,000, besides keeping itself in repair.

This road furnished a very convenient passage for settlers in this new country and westward. Some portions of this part of the State owe their early existence and growth to this road. It gave a decided impulse to the increase of population and improvements to the surrounding country."

NO. IX.

"This road was begun in 1812. It commences at Mount Pleasant, and was to terminate at Dingman's Ferry on the Delaware river, in Pike County—a distance of fifty miles. It was, however, never finished further than its intersection with the Milford and Owego turnpike—a distance of thirty-two miles. The capital stock was $40,000. Private subscriptions, $24,000. State subscription, $8,000. Average cost of the road per mile was $904. The principal objects of the road were—to open a communication to market, chiefly to Philadelphia, by way of the Delaware river—and promote the more rapid settlement of this part of the State. In consequence of great changes in public improvements and modes of travel, it has been relinquished, with the exception of that portion lying between Bethany and Mount Pleasant."

NO. X.

The average yield of Indian corn, under good tillage, is fifty bushels per acre. The cost of raising it is about fifty-two cents per bushel. The soil being highly adapted to grazing, more attention, of late, has been paid to dairying than any other branch of agriculture.

NO. XI.

The following are the names of those who united in the organization of this Church:

SAMUEL STANTON,	MARTHA STANTON,
JOSEPH TANNER,	LYDIA TANNER,
MARGARET DIX,	RHODA STEARNS.

NO. XII.

The following are the names of the communicants on this occasion:—Joseph Tanner, Samuel Stanton, Abram Cramer, Joseph Cromwell, Margaret Dix, Rhoda Stearns, Martha Stanton, Lydia Tanner, and Anna Cramer.

NO. XIII.

This society was the first Temperance Society properly of Wayne County. The Damascus and Cochecton Temperance Society, organized in May, 1829, was located partly in New York State. But nine persons could be induced to join this society, at its organization. It became auxiliary to the Wayne County Temperance Society, in 1832. In 1834, the society took forty copies of "The Temperance Recorder."

INDEX

ACKERMANN, Karen 13
ALLEN, Seymore 35
ARTHUR, Mr 65
ATWATER, Edward M 36
BAIRD, Mr 30
BAKER, Mr 52
BARRAGER, Jacobus 29
BENJAMIN, John 76 Sarah 75
BIGELOW, James H 41 James 41
BONAPARTE, 67
BOYCE, Henry A 60
BOYD, James 58
BREWSTER, 41
BROADHEAD, Mr 77
BROOKING, Samuel 84
BROWN, John 41 T H 29
BUNTIN, John 22
BURNSIDE, Judge 24
CARR, Reuben 52
CHANDLER, Dr 65
CHAPMAN, Robert H 58
CHITTENDEN, Anson Sr 62 Noah 28
CHRISTOPHER, Mr 27 51
COATES, Frederic 17
CONDIT, Aaron 58
COOPER, Mr 10-11 William 10-11
CORNWALLIS, 78
COX, Tench 40

CRAIG, Andrew 11 William 11
CRAMER, Abram 35 59 83 96 Anna 96
CROMWELL, Joseph 96
DEPUIS, Nicholas 53 77
DIX, Benjamin 43 52 Elijah 26 28-29 31 52 54 63 Margaret 96 Mr 28 52
DRINKER, Henry 11
DUER, Mr 38
DYE, Mr 89
EATON, Jacob 62 64
ELDRIDGE, Edwin 66
ELLIS, Benjamin 59
ESSARY, Solomon 65
FRANKLIN, Thomas 11
FREEMAN, Calvally 41
FRENCH, Dr 66 Jonathan 66
GEER, Amasa 28 Mr 52 63 35
GEORGE, II King Of Great Britain 7
GRANER, 43
HAGAR, Christopher 9
HAMILTON, Alexander 38
HARMES, Rodney 66
HIGBIE, Daniel 60
HILBORN, John 10-11
HILLYER, Asa 58
HOOPER, Robert L 55

HORTON, David 84 Gilbert 84
INDIAN, Brant 77
JAYNE, David 57
JEFFERSON, Thomas 39
KELLOGG, Eliphalet 25
  Jerry 26 Mr 25-26 28
  Silas 25 42 44 51 83
KENNEDY, Charles 42 John P 65 N E 94
KING, Benjamin 36 44 52 83
  Charles 37
KINGSBURY, Ebenezer 59
LANE, Mr 10 24
LEONIDAS, 67
LILLIBRIDGE, Lowell 65
  Mrs 13 45 Thomas 42
MATHEWS, Sarah 75
MCMULLEN, Geo 68 70 72
MCREYNOLDS, Anthony 60
MEREDITH, Mr 39 Mrs 40
  Reese 37 Samuel 37-38
MIFFLIN, Thomas 40
MILLER, Alexander 41
  Jonathan Sr 47 Wesley 64
MOASE, George 36
MUMFORD, Deborah 47
  Harry 82-83 Jirah 27-28 30 36 42 Minor 12 27 Mr 27-28 30 48 52 Mrs 47 Sally 47 Thomas 27 82
NEWTON, Benjamin 52
  Henry 52
OSBORNE, Aaron 76 Sarah 76
OWEN, Annon 59
PALMER, Henry L 65
PARKS, Asa 65
PECK, Elijah 35 43 59 67-68 82 George 59 Joseph 35

PENN, Richard 9 Thomas 9 William 9
PERKINS, Richard 64
PRESTON, Judge 22 Mr 10-11 Paul S 89 Samuel 10 20
PUTNAM, Gen 72
READ, Sarah 75 William 75
REEDER, Joseph 83
RICHARDSON, E 26
  Ebenezer 54
ROGERS, Jirah 65 John S 35 Thomas 10-11
ROOD, Nathan 52
ROWLAND, Henry A 33
SAMPSON, Ezekiel 42
SHERWOOD, John F 65
SLAYTON, Thomas 35
SMITH, Asa 28 46 Benjamin 51
SOPER, George 43
SPENCER, Philo 64
STANTON, Asa 17 82
  Martha 96 Mr 10-13 17 20 22 24 26 43 45 47 51-52 55-58 Samuel 10-11 40 42 53 82 89 9 93 96
STARKS, Ichabod 35 Luther 23 82
STEARNS, Ashbel 46 Jabez 42 James 27 Joseph 27 45 51 Lucy 63 Mr 27-28 Otis 27 47 Rhoda 96
STENNETT, 58
STEVENSON, Joseph 35
STONE, Mr 62 William R 62 64 84
TANNER, Joseph 28 42-43 52 64 82 96 Lydia 96 Mr 82 Silas 52 Zebulon 42
THATCHER, Daniel 23 58

THOMPSON, Elder 59
   Epaphras 58 83
TIFFANY, Chandler 82 John
   26 51-52 59 67 82 Mr 67
TORREY, Ephraim 32 Jason
   29 33 45 82 Mr 32-34
   William 32
TRACY, Frederick 66
TYLER, John 63
VAN, Meter Charles 35
   Meter Jacob Sr 42 Meter
   Jacob 35 42
WASHINGTON, Gen 37 78

WEST, Solomon 52
WHALEY, Rev Mr 92
   Samuel 84
WHEELER, Benjamin 37 83
   Charles T 65 Heman J
   25 Truman 64 William H
   65
WHITFIELD, 58
WRIGHT, Dr 66 Uriel 66
   William 51 Worthington
   59
WRIGHTER, John 73

www.ingramcontent.com/pod-product-compliance
Lightning Source LLC
Chambersburg PA
CBHW070321100426
42743CB00011B/2505